THE PUNJABI'S WIFE

LARA LYONS

To Kelli
Be Strong!

From
Laura
3/30/10

"Decisions Lara made as a young woman were based on a romantic belief in honesty and love. The wrenching lessons she learned are universal and priceless"
- **Linda Hatch**, Retired Montana Mental Health Administrator.

"A captivating account of a young woman's journey of self discovery in a foreign land. Vivid and heartbreaking. I couldn't put it down."
- **Robert M. Strumor,** Attorney-at-Law, Santa Fe, New Mexico

"The Punjabi's Wife was so compelling that I could not put it down. I finished the book in one weekend! I was amazed at how this young woman was able to handle such cultural diversity and maintain her mental balance. It was a gripping tale of a girl's transition into womanhood in a world far from her own. I encourage every young woman seeking an adventure to read this book first".
- **Teresa Haft**, Executive Assistant, Exempla, Inc.

"An interesting story of a brave young American girl who experienced life as a Muslim wife - I just couldn't put it down and read it several times."
- **Aaron Janowski**, CEO Wellsley Corporation

THE PUNJABI'S WIFE

ISBN: 0-9822056-8-6
ISBN 13: 978-09822056-8-6
LIBRARY OF CONGRESS NUMBER: 2008942159

Cover design by All Things That Matter Press
Published in 2008 by All Things That Matter Press
Printed in the United States of America

I dedicate this book to my father,
who died in the spring of 2007.
His humor, love, wisdom, and optimism,
even in times of adversity,
gives me much to live up to in life.

Table of Contents

INTRODUCTION

The morning after one of my daughter's weddings in September 1998, I was sitting in a coffee shop at the Oxford Hotel in Denver with a friend, waiting patiently for someone to take our breakfast orders. We were soon approached by a young blond American woman, probably in her early 20's, dressed in traditional light colored Muslim clothes which hid her hair, her entire body to her ankles, and her arms in long sleeves. Her face was uncovered and she offered no smile; her eyes were downcast and she would not meet mine as I looked at her. I involuntarily tensed all over and glanced behind her, sweeping the room for something or someone. I soon spotted a dark, slender, serious man from the Middle East sitting alone at a table on the far side of the café. He watched the waitress's every move, waiting for her to slip up in what could be interpreted as flirting or looking at a male customer.

I immediately knew what was happening to this girl and my anger was building to such a level that it was difficult to control my instant reactions. I wanted to jump up out of my seat and drag the waitress out of the café. With every muscle in my body I would shake some sense into her while screaming for her to get control over her life and run out of this man's domineering reach. Where was her self esteem, her common sense, and what had caused her to allow this person to control her every thought, move and personality?

Memories from my own life flooded back into my thoughts and I could not stay in the café any longer watching this scene of domination and humiliation.

After this incident at the Oxford Hotel, my desire to write about my seven year marriage from 1969 to 1976 to a Muslim man from Pakistan became paramount.

This book is also written for my twin daughters so that they might begin to understand what happened to cause me to marry a man from the other side of the world and some of the reasons I divorced him when they were still very young. It is difficult to write about these years in my life.

I have tried to forget the pain my seven year marriage to this man caused me. In fact, during most of these years I have been afraid to write anything concerning my Muslim husband. I was afraid of what Ali could do to my daughters, afraid of his anger, afraid of his relatives, afraid of his religion. When my daughters were very young, I learned how to use a pistol and took shooting lessons from a police captain I had met in Colorado. Since that time I have always owned guns and keep one or more in the house at all times.

I spent the next four years dragging my memories out of my brain, writing and re-writing about those years and beyond, when I was terrified he would steal my young daughters and take them to Pakistan. I wrenched each incident, each lesson and experience out of the depths of my mind where I had hidden them. I had wild dreams and sleepless nights during this period, but felt that it was important to put these experiences on paper. I wanted desperately to help other women who might flirt with the possibility that they could find romance and love from a distant land with the handsome men who were so intense about life and religion. This was the reason for creating "The Punjabi's Wife" and wanting to have it published.

My own experiences with a Muslim happened thirty-two years before September 11, 2001, but I was not surprised when I watched on CNN the two planes hit the Twin Towers in New York City. I had met people who had the capabilities of this extremist behavior and knew that this act of terrorism was not an isolated incident.

CHAPTER 1: THE FATEFUL MEETING

To get from St. Louis to Karachi, Pakistan, it takes about fourteen hours of flight time with one stop in Abu Dhabi. In December 1968 when the Pan Am flights stopped there for refueling, it was a tiny undeveloped state on the Persian Gulf coast. Still a teenager, I had never taken a trip outside the United States and was panicked about the adventure. The stewardess opened the door of the plane and let passengers go down the metal stairs onto the tarmac. I had no idea where Abu Dhabi was located and was so nervous about missing the plane that I only ventured to the stairs of the craft. My eyes closed to small slits as I squinted toward the sand surrounding the airport. Everything was a bright, glaring white, and I could barely stand to look at it. A wave of hot air blasted into the plane. Shaking and afraid, I could not stop my tears from falling as the stewardess watched. She asked me questions concerning my ultimate destination and distracted me somewhat with her conversation. Napping on the airplane seats was impossible and instead I forced myself to read some Reader's Digest books and a few magazines to calm my wild thoughts. I missed my twin sister and was flying toward an unknown world.

What strange madness had put me in this situation? What would I do if my new husband, Ali, did not show up at the Karachi Airport? I didn't know the language or the customs of the country I was headed toward. I guessed I could go to the American Embassy if I had any problems.

What if I had made a terrible mistake in marrying this man? All of these thoughts ran through my brain continuously as if they were a television show in my head. The United States government gave no instructions when leaving the country on what to do in case of trouble in a foreign land.

The plane landed at Karachi Airport in the middle of the afternoon. There were no fancy walkways, only metal stairs on wheels. As I descended the stairs from the plane, I finally breathed a big sigh of relief! Ali was waiting for me at the bottom. He was dressed in American clothes and greeted me warmly, but whispered that he could not kiss or hug me. I was crying, and he hushed my tears and told me not to worry about anything. No contact between men and women was allowed in a Muslim countries airport's public area. He at once took charge of everything and I was relieved to have him with me.

Why had I left my safe family to visit this strange land? It is interesting to wonder how fate leads you down certain mysterious paths where you suddenly find things are not how you imagined they might be. I had blindly rushed toward this life in Pakistan without knowing anything about the country, the religion, or the history. I certainly did not understand my new husband, and believed he loved me. Here I was, a nineteen year old girl, far away from my native land and family. Now I was totally dependent on this much older man. I began to think I had made a grave mistake, but could not change direction and go home to my mother and father. I was stuck in Pakistan, had no money, and was totally at the mercy of my new husband to protect me and support me. I must try to make the best of the next two years, until I could return to the United States safely.

Innocence can be defined in many different ways, and my twin sister, Lynne, and I were definitely innocent in our freshman year at Southern Illinois University in Carbondale. The year was 1967, and in June we were eighteen and one half years old. Our futures lay ahead of us and our eagerness to search for knowledge and adventure seemed overwhelming. Both of us were straining at the leash to leave home, but we needed reasons to do so and income to make it practical. It was an era in America when most teenagers of our generation were anxious to leave home and find ways of supporting themselves. The restrictive environment of family life in Midwestern America and the strict morals from the World War II generation of parents and grandparents were not what we wanted to believe for ourselves.

Many young people hoped to start making their own decisions immediately, and my sister and I were no exception. This feeling may have been caused by the excessive sheltering, our own maturity level, or something else unexplainable that none of us completely understood, but felt deeply. We were eager to try just about anything despite being unprepared for life. Yes, we stumbled along the way in making our decisions, but they were ours alone to make and we learned about life from them.

After graduating from two separate local high schools, we immediately started our university classes in the summer semester. We both quickly found jobs working at the university library putting away books, filing documents and photos on the humanities floor. It was easy work for us and we found many interesting, risqué books in the library stacks that our English teacher mother had not told us existed. Thinking back on those years, it is easy to say that we were pretty naïve about how life really was lived in other societies and even in the big cities of America. We were young girls raised in a southern Missouri town most of our lives with our parents and grandparents sheltering us from the hazards of life. But I was soon to become enlightened by many interesting experiences that I had never imagined as an unsophisticated child growing up in Cape Girardeau, Missouri.

While shelving books around the humanities floor of the library, I stumbled over shocking photos of naked men and women, read stories depicting gay sex, and tales involving older, lascivious men taking advantage of young girls, all in the realm of fiction. The humanities floor was large and as I rolled my book cart around, I would have hours to look through many different books and magazines. These were tantalizing images for me and going to work was enjoyable.

Some of these new reading materials opened up my small world to places I had never seen before. Oh, yes, I had stared at those copies of National Geographic on the book shelves of my grandmother when I was ten or eleven years old and wondered about those African women with bare breasts. But what I found on the humanities floor of the library was totally different from the National Geographic. Travel books packed with photos of foreign countries and natives dressed in colorful clothes were engrossing topics for me. These opportunities to study photos of foreign countries and read about world history started me dreaming of exotic places and other civilizations. As naive young girls from Missouri, we had not learned anything about exotic foreign places in high school.

The humanities librarian found me looking at photos several times in the long rows of book stacks and instructed me to move on and finish my job quickly. I managed to continue to read, learn, and dream about the world outside Illinois and the United States even though the eagle eyed librarian watched me closely. This reprimand by the librarian just made me want to do my reading a little more stealthily than before I was caught. Stepping up my speed in the rounds with the library cart still allowed me to find and read the titillating literature that had been denied me at my rather puritanical home.

Within a few months, my sister, Lynne started dating a man from Beirut, Lebanon. In 1967 Beirut was referred to as the "Paris" of the Middle East. It was a cosmopolitan city with a mixture of the French, European and Arab influences blended together to make it one of the only important, stable democracies in the Arab world. It was an old, beautiful city with a large American university and variety of cultural activities and liberal thinking among residents. The Christian Lebanese were particularly influenced by the French who were given Beirut at the end of World War I by the League of Nations. During the years from 1920 until the French withdrew in 1946, Beirut absorbed many European elements, including architecture, language, and viewpoints. From 1975 through 1990, a civil war in Lebanon resulted in vast devastation of Beirut and a division of the city with the Christian majority in East Beirut and Lebanese Sunni Muslims in West Beirut. Some scholars say that the Lebanese Civil War was caused by the militant Palestinian Liberation Organization (PLO) moving into southern Lebanon. Southern Beirut was dominated by Shiite Muslims, Lebanon's poorest community, who suffered from overcrowding due to high birth rates, lack of housing, and the regular influx of Shiites fleeing the violence of southern Lebanon which bordered Israel. Many of these refugees came from Palestinian refugee camps. Over the years of civil war, Beirut was practically leveled by fighting between the Muslim and the Christian populations. There have historically been fierce battles between Islam and other religions, often based on Muhammad's revelation that Allah wanted the entire world to follow Islam.

Even today, Beirut has not rebounded to its former glory, beauty, or educational levels the citizens experienced before the Lebanese civil war. Lebanon is relatively quiet now and there appears to be a process of reconstruction going on that might help the political situation and encourage economic growth. Recent political assassinations and renewed sporadic fighting has again caused the population, both Muslim and Christian to wonder about their economic future.

The Lebanese man's name was Pierre and he was a Catholic instead of a Muslim. This religious difference meant he was from the elite society in Lebanon and his education and manners were to be admired. Pierre had many friends, mostly Middle Eastern or Arabic men who spoke to him in English or French and knew his culture. On the surface, religion did not seem to matter during this time in their lives. They were students at an American university, and just having friends with similar backgrounds was enough for them. The men would all retreat to the student center to drink coffee, play pool, and discuss politics of the Middle East. Of course, they flirted non-stop with American college girls, hoping to date a few of them. Pierre told us that he came from a wealthy family in Lebanon. I don't know if this was just bragging on his part, or reality. He was engaged to a Lebanese woman he had grown up with in Beirut. Their two families were close, and it was expected that he marry the girl upon his return to Beirut. However, this engagement did not stop him from dating my twin sister.

Some of the foreign men did not talk about their families back in the Middle Eastern countries, and if they talked about them, they spoke about their lives in a positive manner or said what they believed the American girls wanted to hear. Some married men told American girls they had wives back in their native lands and some did not mention it to anyone. I was told at a later time that many Muslim men believed American women to be promiscuous and if the foreign men flirted with them they might get free sex if they kept quiet about their personal lives.

Many impressions about American women were created through Hollywood movies and some television shows that were shown around the world. Often these shows, while mild to us in America, shocked the Muslim world and gave the wrong perception to those who viewed them. If an unmarried woman in a Muslim country wore heavy make-up and flirted with or slept with men, they were considered prostitutes and whores. No man would marry them after their flamboyant displays, and their families would shun them for the rest of their lives. Muslim women who had sex with a married man could be stoned or shot for adultery, even if she did not know the man was married or even if she had been raped by a married man.

Pierre spoke French, English, Arabic, and Lebanese fluently and was suave. Lynne fell for him and often went to his apartment for hours when not in class or at work. This amorous adventure was kept secret from everyone in our family except me, and because Lynne and I had to share an old red Renault car to get to school, we would often rendezvous at the student center to ride home together after work.

We both worked in the university library humanities department and would put in hours at different times of the day and evening, between our classes or study time. One night after work, about 9:00 o'clock, I was wandering the halls of the university student center looking for Lynne and ended up in the activity room where the pool tables were located. Sitting near one of the pool tables were many foreign men, and one of them approached me to ask if he could read my palm. No one had ever offered to tell my future by reading my palm, so I extended my hand for him to hold. I was aware that this was a pick-up line created to encourage girls to be friendly with him, but it was creative and I was amused by his attempt. I played the game and flirted sweetly with him just for fun. He proceeded to read a glorious fortune for me while carefully holding and looking at my right, up-turned palm. His name was Ali Sayeed and he was ten to fifteen years older than me. He was studying communications and trying to finish his Ph.D. thesis before he returned to Pakistan. He quickly found out that he was flirting with a freshman student who had no idea of what to do in life. The way the foreign men looked at me told me that they all thought I was pretty and hoped they could get a date, but Ali was the only one who came forward and began the conversation.

Ali and I played pool for about an hour until Lynne and Pierre showed up at the activity room after one of their trysts. It was late at night and we had to get home or mother would be mad at us, so we quickly left the men. Ali had my name and phone number and my work schedule at the library. He had carefully extracted this information out of me during our game of pool. I did not know if he would continue our conversation or even try to find me again, but it would be interesting to find out if he did want to see me.

Soon after that evening, Ali came up to the humanities floor in the library to find me at work, shelving books. It was flattering when he followed me around the floor and asked me if we could meet for coffee later in the day. As a graduate student, he had a carrel to work in the library basement and was busy writing his doctoral thesis. As time passed and I got to know him better, I would join him down in the library basement so we could go for food or coffee at the student center which was only about a ten minute walk from the library. Later in the fall semester of 1967 we would meet at his carrel and spend time kissing or "making out" until some other graduate student entered the locked, restricted area.

Ali was a Muslim from the Punjab region of West Pakistan, but for me to understand what this meant in those early days of our relationship would have taken hours of study about that part of the world. He was approximately 29 to 34 years old in 1967, but no one really knew his exact age because at the time he was born records were not kept on births. Children were born at home and no doctors or officials bothered to issue birth certificates. Many children died of disease and accidents, so the first real records on these children started later in life, usually when they began school. Ali's mother was illiterate and made approximations on his birth date, but there was no birth certificate or any other document which would give me the real date for of his birth. He had estimated the date to get his Pakistani passport, and no one in Pakistan cared if it was a real date or just fabricated.

He was approximately 5'8" tall and had broad shoulders with large muscles. Ali claimed to have studied certain self defense modes like Judo and wrestling, but I only saw him do very slight defense maneuvers from time to time. His hair was jet black, thick, and wavy. He had a pleasant face with absolutely perfect white teeth. When he laughed, which was often, his teeth flashed in a big smile. He bragged many times that he had never visited a dentist and never had a cavity. He described how in Pakistan they used a particular twig from a tree to brush his teeth since he was a child. His theory was that this twig had some medicinal properties which helped his teeth stay cavity free. It always sounded like a pretty vague personal hygiene story to me and I believed his dental perfection to be genetic. Ali always tried to be charming and resorted to kissing the hand of my mother when he finally met her, even though this was taboo in his own country. I am sure he picked this affectation up from some foreign movie he had seen while in America and thought it would endear women to him. My mother was extremely flattered and taken off guard by the hand kissing gesture.

Ali was born in Lahore, India, sometime between 1932 and 1937. At that time the English ruled India and did not leave until 1947 after many years of negotiations, riots, and deaths. For many years before this, Mahatma Gandhi had issued calls for independence from British rule and became famous for his non-violent resistance against the British. Without Gandhi's famous courage and non-violent beliefs the British might not have left India on August 15, 1947. He was considered the architect of Indian independence and father of the nation. Immediately after the English moved out of India there was a great "partition" of India and Pakistan which was extremely violent. Hindu and Sikh refugees had streamed into the capital city of Delhi, fleeing the region that had become Pakistan. There was much resentment between the religions in India. This resentment easily translated into violence against Muslims who were moving to the newly created Pakistan. The Punjab, called "land of the five rivers", was an important part of this partition, and was split between the two countries. Many Muslim Punjabis were slaughtered by Hindus and Sikhs. The Muslims also hideously murdered many Hindus during this time. There are stories of dead mutilated women, children, and men lying on trains going between the two countries. Partition may have taken the lives of as many as one million people, besides causing the relocation of no fewer than eleven million people. The region of Kashmir was in dispute and still, to this day, one hears often of violent clashes between Muslim rebels and Indian soldiers there.

Ali must have been very young at the time of the partition and might have remembered the bloody origins of his native West Pakistan. If he had these memories he never mentioned any trouble from his childhood to me. But he often prided himself on being part of the history of the Punjab and its very war-like population. Ali's father, Mohammed Sharif, had been killed during World War II fighting for the British in Africa. A photo of him I once viewed showed a tall, handsome man, with a large mustache, dressed in an army uniform. I was told that his singing voice was beautiful, but that none of his children had inherited his voice. Ali had been born into a middle class family in Lahore, Pakistan. He was the youngest son of the family. His older brother, Salim, was married and currently had ten sons and one daughter. His older sister, Shafia, was married and living in England with her husband and two children. Shafia's husband, Ahmed, was her first cousin. Because his mother was a widow and had no husband to care for her, she lived with Ali's older brother, Salim, and helped care for his children and clean his house. She was referred to as Mahji, meaning respected mother, and was extremely religious, praying five times per day on her prayer rug facing Mecca.

Ali had received several Masters Degrees from Punjab University and had come to America in an exchange program with Indiana University. He received a Masters degree at Indiana and then transferred to Southern Illinois University to work on a Ph.D. degree in Communications. Now at Carbondale, he had only about a year to finish his studies, write his thesis, and return to Lahore to teach at Punjab University. He had a contract with the university that forced him to return to Pakistan to teach for no less than two years before leaving. I was told they paid for his trip to America and tuition at both of the universities he attended in the United States. He owed two years of teaching to the University of the Punjab, in Lahore, but was trying to finish his doctorate first. Ali was quickly running out of time.

While in Carbondale, Ali lived in a very small rental cabin near the campus. The cabin was located in the back yard of his landlord's home. This cabin looked like it had been used for storage of some kind and then re-modeled into a rental unit to take advantage of the shortage of student housing at that time in Carbondale. It had a twin bed, a chair, a small kitchen with table and stove, and a bathroom in the back. The bathroom had only a toilet, sink, and small shower.

I lived at home with my parents, twin sister, and older brother in this small university town. We had found a two story house in a new subdivision at the edge of Carbondale in which to live. Many university professors were buying houses in this part of town, and homes cost approximately $25,000 to $35,000 depending upon their size and style. Many of the streets in this area looked alike, with sidewalks and street lamps carefully laid out by the contractor who built the subdivision.

My mother and father had moved us from Cape Girardeau, Missouri, where we were born, to Carbondale, Illinois in 1965, so my mother could attend the university to get her Master's degree in English Literature. It was also considered a good move for my older brother, who would attend the university at about the same time as a sophomore. Cape Girardeau, Missouri is a town approximately two hours south of St. Louis located directly on the Mississippi River. My mother was raised there and my grandparents and extended family also lived in Cape. The town's population in 1967 was approximately 20,000 people, and my mother always used to tell me that there was a large German population in town, which made it conservative. My grandfather was of German heritage and my grandmother's family was Scotch Irish. There was a poor side of town where the Black population lived, and some of the Negro women had worked for my mother and grandmother as housekeepers when I was growing up. My great grandmothers are both buried in the cemeteries of Cape Girardeau, and most of my mother's ancestors came from Southeastern Missouri. My father was from Minnesota, but raised in Nebraska, and had met my mother during World War II. They were married in Cape Girardeau in 1944. Moving to Carbondale was a financial stretch for our family, but we somehow managed it with the help of my maternal grandfather.

My twin sister and I attended two separate high schools for two years after we moved to Carbondale before we graduated. We wanted the opportunity to feel what it was like to be treated as separate individuals instead of twins. We both started the university immediately after high school graduation in June of 1967. We had never met anyone from foreign lands and the Middle East was a complete mystery to both of us.

My twin sister and I were about 5'7" tall, slender blond Midwestern girls. We were intelligent, had a certain charm, and were reasonably attractive. It was the middle of the 1960's and the world was changing rapidly. The sexual revolution was beginning to transform how college students thought and acted. The next decade would change the direction of the world and liberate women from old traditions and expectations. I'm sure it was difficult for our parents and grandparents to understand these changes that were occurring so rapidly. My mother's sister often said that Carbondale, Illinois was a "hot bed of communist activity". This statement was meant to explain why her own daughters would not be allowed to attend any out-of-state college and instead went to the local South East Missouri State College where my aunt had attended school for a few years, never finishing her degree. It was also meant to be a negative comment thrown at my mother and father for moving us to Carbondale where all the foreigners were going to school. What my Aunt did not know was that all colleges and universities in the 1960's and 1970's were hot beds of some sort. My sister and I were naïve and desperately trying to get into some of the action that was happening around us. We wanted to experience everything we could in our young lives, including sex. Eager for freedom from tradition, the small town experience, and a new life made us inquisitive. The handsome, dark, foreign men we met were exotic and intriguing to us. They represented the unknown world, things we had not been taught or seen before. They were men and not the boys of our youth. We imagined exotic life styles from novels or movies, and we were probably easy prey for these men's attentions.

I am not entirely sure why I went out with Ali the first few times. As I think back on my life it is hard to imagine that a Missouri girl could be so foolish. I do remember that I was not particularly attracted to him physically, but could not ignore his flattering attentions to me. Over time I became impressed with his education and in love with his differences and worldly experiences. His sexual attentions and exotic background were different than the local boys I had dated in high school. These small town boys knew nothing of the world or romance and did not pursue me with any kind of zest or enthusiasm. They were busy with their families, sports, and male friends, while girl friends were just given a few hours for a date once or twice per week. Ali made me his personal priority. He had no family in America and his only friends were other men from the Middle Eastern countries. His time was either devoted to study and writing of his thesis or vigorously chasing me. Of course, at this time I did not know of his desire to marry an American girl so he could get a visa and return to the United States after two years teaching in Pakistan.

I was not innocent regarding sex at the time of my meeting Ali. During my last year of high school in Carbondale, I had fleeting sexual liaisons in the back seat of my high school boy friend's car. I remember that I always wanted more than these types of sexual trysts because this tall, handsome young man was captain of the football team and son of a college professor. However, he was brought up conservatively by his strict Presbyterian parents and was critical of me. His parents were religious and he told me that sex outside of marriage was sinful. Apparently not so sinful that he stopped his advances, he just felt guilty for it afterward. Of course, I was always afraid of becoming pregnant. In 1967 girls were kept ignorant about birth control, but we all knew there were condoms available in the men's restroom at the local bowling alley. So I demanded that my boy friend stop at the bowling alley before we went out parking on country roads. My mother never explained much to me about sex because she had lectured us on how "good girls" act and expected us to be virgins until we wed. I am not sure if my mother or grandmother ever understood the sexual revolution of the 60's and 70's or how it liberated young women.

As Ali and I talked more about his life during these early days of our dating, I learned some things about his youth and the country of Pakistan. He told me stories of a beautiful girl, Jasmine; he had fallen in love with in his early 20's. She was a distant relative, a second or third cousin, whom he wanted to marry, but both families were against the match because he had no money. The couple tried to run away together at one time but somehow her family found out about it and stopped the elopement. Jasmine's family later arranged a marriage to someone else and Ali lost contact with her. They never had sex, and probably never even kissed each other, but she was the lost love of his life. When he talked about her it was obvious that he would never forget this particular girl. Of course, the story was romantic, sad, and told me something about the arranged marriages of Muslim countries. It did not matter what the girl wanted, but only what her parents had decided for her was important in an arranged marriage. Many times the girls lived a harsh, brutal life with a man they did not love, like, or even respect.

In 1967 Pakistan was a different country than it is today. The British has been in India since 1600 and it had a huge impact on culture there. Many people spoke English as a second language, and the extremist Muslim Mullahs and Imams had very little power. Many British ideas and customs had taken hold in the hundreds of years of occupation in India. The hatred for America that is currently preached in the Middle East did not exist in 1968. There was a definite loathing for Israel by many Pakistanis during these years, and this still holds true to this day. The Israelis had shown their strength and determination to the entire world during the six day Arab/Israeli conflict in June 1967. Anti-Semitism and hatred was pervasive in the Pakistan/Muslim culture and the rest of the Middle Eastern Arab countries. America was perceived as a rich distant country full of blond Christian women by many Middle Eastern people. It was considered much like Britain in culture, but different because America had the CIA that aggressively infiltrated every foreign country. Except for the fear of the mysterious CIA, most young men and women from Pakistan wanted to visit or live in America to take advantage of the financial opportunities and prospering economy. The U-2 reconnaissance spy plane that was shot down over Russia with the pilot, Francis Gary Powers, in May 1960 had flown from a Turkish air base. Many people in Pakistan felt sure that it was a CIA plane and that it compromised their relationship with the USSR. Pakistanis talked as if the plane had flown from somewhere in their country, and it was a topic of discussion often between men even eight years later when I lived there.

Ali told me about his adventures in a Pakistani mafia before he traveled to the United States. Ali liked to gamble, mostly at cards, and during card games he met a "Godfather" who held major control over a large gambling ring. These people would cheat and steal from

23

unsuspecting men who gambled at cards. Ali was recruited by the Godfather to be part of a rough gang. This happened after he lost the woman he loved, and in his depression he joined the gang to help pay for his education. He was taught how to cheat at cards and showed me some of the tricks he would use. Slight of hand, double dealing, and dealing off the bottom of the deck were his methods of winning. To me, these maneuvers were pretty impressive magic tricks, but I did not think of them as criminal. I was not connecting yet with the fact that these were all indications of his lack of moral character and that he had cheated many people since he was in his early 20's to make money for his life style. I never heard a story of him getting a job or working for his money.

When we were dating he often went to play cards with his six or eight Pakistani and Indian friends. They would always play for money, and invariably Ali won. He would show me fists full of cash that he had cheated his friends out of during a card game. I was never allowed to attend these card games and he never spent the money on me or on presents. He must have had a growing bank account, because when he returned to Pakistan he bought and shipped back a Volkswagen, a refrigerator, and many presents for all his family, plus business suits for himself and his brother. I suspected much of this money came from his extensive gambling, but I was never sure.

As time went on during my freshman year at the university, Ali and I spent more time together. We would go to dinner at his foreign friend's homes and eat Indian and

Pakistani food. We never went to movies or restaurants for a date, probably because these activities cost money and he did not want to spend any of his ill gotten gains. I would visit his small cabin and he would cook chicken and rice for me sometimes. He told me that chicken was very expensive in Pakistan and the desired food by many people. We would eat dinner and then he would seduce me in his twin bed. I remember the smell of spices, onions, curry, and cardamom in his cabin, sometimes overwhelming after these dinners. I did not use birth control yet because I was afraid to go to the student health center as an unmarried girl and ask for the pill. I guess we were taking real chances, but we did not make love often. When we did have sex, Ali tried to use the "withdrawal" method of birth control. At the time we did not know that withdrawal was not an efficient way to prevent pregnancy.

During these days Ali was often studying or gambling, and I had classes and work to keep me busy. He would sometimes call me at home from the university library pay phone in the evening, and I would borrow the car to drive to meet him, either at the university or his small cabin. My parents usually thought I was studying in the library or working at my job. I don't believe they ever realized what I was doing those late nights. In the early days of our romance, Ali never came to my house to pick me up or for dinner. He avoided meeting my parents for many months. He did not have a car or phone at his small house at this time and lived within walking distance of the university. He had a graduate assistantship and was constantly working on his Ph.D. thesis, but never finished it.

In December 1967 I became ill with a virus of some kind, probably the flu. Staying home, in bed, with a high fever and horrible mouth sores, it was hard for me even to talk during this illness. My mother took me to the University Medical Center twice trying to find some cure. The doctors said I had a virus and there was nothing to do for it but rest and drink plenty of liquids until the virus went away. They told us antibiotics would not help my mouth sores, so I received no medicine. During this period, Ali called me many times and I told him I could not see him because of my illness. After two weeks, he started getting angry with me, feeling I was avoiding him and not really ill.

When he finally saw me again after three weeks he was very surprised, and realized by looking at the remaining fever blisters and my weight loss that I had really been ill. His reaction was interesting and sympathetic for my pain. He told me that in Pakistan when someone was severely sick they usually cut off all their hair. I could not understand what hair had to do with any illness, but Ali said that it just grew back in stronger afterward

CHAPTER 2: THE FIRST WEDDING

Our marriage took place at the local Methodist Church on July 11, 1968, but the months leading up to the ceremony were filled with hysterical fights with my mother and some misunderstandings with Ali.

Sometime in February 1968, Ali asked if I wanted to get married and move to Pakistan with him. He was being forced to leave the country because of his student visa restrictions. January was my 19th birthday and I did not need permission from my parents to get married, but went to them and announced my intensions. My mother became practically hysterical and tried to talk me out of the marriage with Ali. I specifically remember one night after work when I came home about 9:00 o'clock, she called me into her bedroom to tell me a story about when she was young and had fallen in love with a New York doctor's son. They had a terrible fight over some petty incident and he left her to begin dating one of her girl friends. She was heartbroken over this experience, but, after some time, met my wonderful father and married him. The story was supposed to show me that you can find happiness with others and don't have to marry your first love.

At the time, my mother's story was very confusing; through all her tears and nose blowing efforts its meaning was unclear to me. Its relevance to my particular situation was hard to fathom, and I told her I did not care what she was trying to tell me; the marriage was still on with Ali. To this day I remember perfectly what her bedroom looked like that particular night. My father was not home yet, and mother was in bed with her nightgown on, crying. A box of Kleenex tissues, almost totally used up, was sitting beside her on the bed. A small lamp was turned on and the light shown in a circle around her. She had me sit close to her and as she cried she told me the story of her young broken heart. Trying to comfort her just turned into a fight between us. Within minutes I ended up leaving the bedroom and going to my own room down the hallway.

We did not discuss my marriage to Ali again after that particular fight. She knew I meant business and was not going to be swayed by her tears and pleadings concerning whether I was too young to know my own mind or any other reason she might have to stop me from going through with the wedding. She had upset me terribly by suggesting that Ali did not love me, but was only marrying me to gain American citizenship. I did not want to believe that he was deceiving me, and tried to put these thoughts out of my mind.

During these years, my father was a salesman and Dictaphone repairman. He traveled most of the time around Southern Illinois to visit various customers. The family did not see much of father because of his constant traveling. We did not have much money, especially with three kids in college at the same time. All of us had to work just to pay our tuition to the university. The house they had purchased in Carbondale cost more than they wanted to spend, but somehow they were able to swing the loan. About the time I met Ali; mother had just finished her master's degree and gotten a job teaching at the local high school. She taught for about one year and had a disagreement with her supervisor and left the position in disgust. It upset her terribly and she kept saying that there was no discipline in the Carbondale high schools. After that particular job, she began to teach English as a second language for foreign students part-time at the university. She was about 45 years old and went through several years of crying and depression, not because of me, but for reasons she could not explain easily. She visited a university counselor for a while, but it did not seem to help her moods. I don't remember if she was prescribed any drugs, or if so, we children did not know about it. I do remember that she never told us anything about her thoughts, aspirations, dreams, or problems. We three grown children were concentrating on leaving home and making our own way in the world during those years. We were not much comfort to our suffering mother. She had to deal with these changes in her life all by herself, because father was on the road so much. Our ultimate defection may have contributed to her depression during these years, or maybe she was just reviewing her own life direction.

After many arguments and tears, my parents began to accept how stubborn I could be and that I had made up my mind to marry Ali, so we began planning a wedding to take place before he left the country. Ali came to dinner a few times at our house and we even took him on the two hour trip to Cape Girardeau to meet my grandparents and the rest of the family. Relatives also traveled to Carbondale to meet him at least one time. It was quite a shock to most of them, because they had never met a person from the Middle East, and Ali had dark skin. My mother felt she had to explain several times to all the relatives that Ali was not a Negro, but a Caucasian with dark skin. I was embarrassed each time she made this explanation to her family and friends. I had never thought of Ali as a Black person, and I felt she was apologizing for his skin color in front of everyone.

My grandparents were in their late 60's and had been both raised in Southern households. Their attitude toward anyone with dark skin was prejudiced, but they kept their opinions to themselves and were gracious toward Ali when they finally met him. My aunt also kept her opinions to herself during these times and did not refuse him hospitality in her home. I remember my Grandmother Quinn's shock and dismay when she first heard of our wedding plans. My mother had called her and announced it one evening when I was not at home. She later told me how disappointed my grandparents had acted over my decision to marry so young.

I am sure my mother heard many recriminations from her elderly parents about this marriage during these months before the wedding. I cried a lot during those months, too, and have unhappy memories of this entire period of time. All of the negativity displayed toward the idea of my marriage to a foreigner made me even more determined to wed him. If they had not been so negative about the marriage to this man, I might have backed out for my own reasons, but to do so because of their displeasure was not in my plans. My twin sister and I had a strong streak of stubbornness in us that had been built up over many years and probably came from our German grandfather. We would both do as we wished no matter what the cost to our selves or our family's happiness. This could have been because of the upheaval in American society at this time or just our youth and desire to leave home to begin our own lives without parents trying to control us.

One time Ali announced to my parents that if they could talk me into calling off the wedding he would understand and leave quietly. This statement placed all the responsibility for the affair on my shoulders and caused me much pain and anguish. Feeling as if I alone must have the strength for the marriage gave me the first indication that there was little love on his part. I also thought that this was his own way of proving that he could exert his control over me   I knew I was being manipulated by Ali and he was trying to force me to change my parent's attitudes toward the wedding.

Because of my parents prejudice and my stubbornness I did not back out of the marriage, but went full speed ahead. No amount of crying or reasoning with family members could change my thoughts about this marriage for any reason. Thinking rationally at this point was difficult, so I blindly followed Ali's plan for the marriage before he left the country. Once or twice during my engagement my parents made the suggestion that Ali was only marrying me so that later on he could easily become an American citizen.   I ignored their suggestion that Ali did not love me and was only using me for his return to America at a later time. In hindsight, I realize that this was exactly what Ali was planning and that he never cared for me or my feelings.

Ali and I found some cheap wedding rings at the local discount jewelry store in a new shopping center near Carbondale. They were matching rings, but cost only about $75 each. Ali said he would not buy anything more expensive and would not consider an engagement ring. He did mention that in Pakistan we would get 22kt gold jewelry with beautiful gem stones. He didn't believe that any jewelry in America could ever compare to the heavy gold and jewels from Pakistan. After I saw the beautiful 22kt gold jewelry later in Lahore, I began to agree with him that Pakistani jewelry is substantially more beautiful.

My parents had to get a loan from the bank to pay for the small wedding and reception. The reception was going to be at our house in the large living room. My aunt sewed the wedding dress and my sisters' bride's maid dress as her wedding gift to me. Both dresses had short skirts, were sleeveless and light weight because of the time of year. My dress was made of white lace and my sister's dress was of very light yellow material. Mother made a veil for the wedding dress and we bought matching shoes. I did not know it at the time, but I am sure Ali was scandalized by the wedding dresses because they revealed so much of our arms and legs. However, he made no mention of the dress design to any of us. A good Muslim woman would not have revealed her arms or legs to the male dominated public. He did not keep any photographs of the wedding or reception to show his relatives in Pakistan, and never ask me to mail any photos to him when he left the country. This was not only because of the scandalous wedding dresses, but also because he never wanted anyone in Pakistan to know he had married me in a Christian ceremony.

Ali asked a young Pakistani friend named Aziz Osman to be his best man. Aziz was also one of the men that Ali played cards with and had beaten with his many card tricks, but Aziz knew nothing of Ali's cheating at cards. A rehearsal dinner was held the night before the wedding that my grandparents paid for at a local restaurant. At the dinner my grandfather, Carl, read a Gaelic prayer of blessing as a toast to the wedding couple:

"May the road rise to meet you,
may the wind be always at your back,
may the sun shine warm on your face,
the rain fall softly on your fields,
and until we meet again,
may God hold you in the palm of his hand."

Tears flowed down my face, but I don't believe Ali understood the significance of the blessing. I had always been my Grandfather's favorite granddaughter, and this marriage was a big disappointment for him. He was doing the best he could to try to show that his love was still intact no matter what I did or where I went in the world. I believe that he and my grandmother, Quinn, were both worried about what would happen to me in Pakistan.

Ali's plan was to be married and immediately fly to New York City, where, after a few days for a honeymoon, I would return to Carbondale and he would proceed on to Europe and Pakistan. His older sister, Shafia, lived in England and he was planning a stop over to visit her on his way home. He also intended to do some shopping for his family in Europe when he was traveling through the area. He said that household items were cheaper in Europe and could be shipped to Pakistan easily.

I would continue my education for one more semester at the university, save enough money for a plane ticket, and in December, 1968, fly to Karachi Pakistan to meet Ali. One of his stated reasons behind this plan was that neither Ali nor I had enough money to purchase the second ticket for me to accompany him immediately. The real reason for this delay in my joining him became obvious to me sometime later. Ali needed to go ahead of me to have time to prepare his Muslim family for the coming of an American bride. In Pakistan, any non-Muslims are treated as second class citizens and not accepted socially by anyone who knows they are Christian. It is to be assumed that most people from England and America are not Muslims and therefore can be discriminated against without any legal or ethical recourse.

However, if a husband could say that his new Christian bride had converted to Islam, then everyone was jubilant that another infidel had seen the light. I was not aware of this fact when preparing for my Methodist wedding in Carbondale, and Ali was not required to change his religion before our marriage. Forced conversion to Christianity was not important to me, and to ask him to believe in any religion that was different than how he had been raised was against my own personal beliefs. He obviously had no intention of telling me what life could be like in a Muslim country for an American, Christian woman. He did not even ask me ahead of time if I would be willing to become a Muslim when I reached Pakistan. Ali kept his plans concerning my imminent conversion to Islam and its beliefs to himself during our engagement and Christian wedding. Had I been given the option ahead of time to convert to Islam I would have laughed about the idea? Understanding of the world's religions was not one of my strong points in those days. I would begin later to understand Islam much too well.

It turned out that Ali had plenty of money and somehow arranged and paid cash for a Volkswagen Beetle car in Germany. He also purchased a kitchen refrigerator, reel to reel tape recorder, and some English wool cloth for suits to bring back to Pakistan, and enjoyed a nice trip through Europe on the way home. Much of the money which paid for his trip was raised from Ali's cheating at cards while he was in America. Of course, I asked no questions and did as instructed by my future husband. I was learning quickly how to obey him instead of my parents. I worked hard to make enough money for the plane ticket and extra supplies to send to Pakistan, never realized that Ali was lying to me about money and living conditions.

We were married in a Methodist ceremony on a warm July morning and then returned to my parent's home for the reception. Before my father walked me down the aisle at the flower filled Methodist church, he once again told me I could back out of the wedding even at this late moment. I answered that I had no intention of stopping the wedding now. Lynne and Aziz walked down the aisle first and then Ali and I followed them to the altar. My twin sister stood next to me while the Methodist preacher performed the ceremony. Ali and I exchanged rings and made our vows and then the ceremony was over. The church was filled with relatives and my parent's friends watching as Ali and I were married by a Methodist preacher.

My mother informed me later that my grandfather, Carl, had cried like a baby during the entire ceremony. I had not seen a single one of his tears, but the thought upset me. Immediately after the ceremony, we signed the marriage certificate and then we were driven to our house and changed into travel clothes. People were coming to the wedding reception and we had only a few hours left in Carbondale before driving to St. Louis and then flying to New York City. My relatives and some of my parent's friends were at the house bringing some presents to the reception. Ali had invited a few Pakistani friends that he knew in Carbondale to come to the wedding and the reception at my parent's home. There was one couple consisting of the Pakistani husband and an American wife who we had met a few times before and even been to their house for dinner. The Pakistani husband immediately found the red wine served by my grandfather and started drinking until his American wife dragged him out of the house. I guess good Muslims can drink wine in America when few other Muslims are watching them. We had a small wedding cake and opened a few presents while chatting with the guests filling my parent's home.

Finally it was time to say goodbye to our guests and get Ali's and my suit cases to take on our honeymoon trip. At approximately 3:00 o'clock in the afternoon my parents and twin sister drove us two hours to St. Louis's Lambert Field. I kissed everyone goodbye and we boarded an airplane for New York City. I had never flown on a plane or been to New York before this flight. I was nervous, but had Ali with me to hold my hand and assure me the plane would stay in the air.

Ali's old landlords were Italian and many of their relatives lived in New York. He had promised that we would visit their relatives while we were there. He did not discuss any of these arrangements with me ahead of time. We arrived in New York at 9:00 o'clock at night and immediately took a cab to the landlord's relative's small apartment in Queens. This was a poor, dark, ugly neighborhood, and the apartment smelled of garlic and was quite small. Worst of all, the Italian relatives did not seem to understand that this was our honeymoon, and they just wanted to chat, feed us sticky candy, and hear about their Carbondale family members. The father of the family was about 65 years old and sitting in a wheelchair. He had diabetes and insisted on telling us about his many health complaints. We sat in their cramped living room on our wedding night until after midnight talking with their family. My mind was reeling with the happenings of the day and despair that it was ending in this miserable apartment. I could not believe that Ali would do this to me on this important night. A quick visit would have been fine with these people, but it was overwhelming for me to sit through this long drawn out misery.

After midnight, I begged to leave and go to a hotel to rest. My emotions were frayed and I was exhausted, both emotionally and physically. At about 2:00 o'clock in the morning we finally ended up at a small, dingy hotel room on "Gun Metal Road" somewhere in Queens, New York. I later heard stories of gangster shootings along this same stretch of road during its long violent history. When we finally got to the motel and were checked into our small and cramped honeymoon room, I crumbled into our narrow bed sobbing. I explained to Ali that I was miserable and disappointed with the situation he was forcing me to experience. Screaming at Ali, I told him about his lack of consideration for me to ever consider visiting those people on our wedding trip. Ali looked at me as if I was crazy and he could not understand why I was crying about a visit with his friend's relatives. I was too upset and worn out to allow him to make love to me that night. We both went to bed irritated and annoyed with each other.

Our wedding night was supposed to be romantic, and instead it was a nightmare for me. I ended up emotionally drained because my dream was shattered so soon in our relationship. Ali had handled the honeymoon plans and I had assumed it would be romantic and beautiful. It really did not matter to him if I had an enjoyable honeymoon; he was thoughtless about my feelings. I looked at it as a very bad omen for the beginning of our lives together.

My older brother was living in New York at this time and we met him briefly the next day. We did not tell him about the previous evening of my unhappy visit in Queens and the bad hotel. We acted like tourists and visited a few art museums and historic sites, but the atmosphere did not change, and when I flew back to St. Louis alone the next day, I was relieved to have finished the honeymoon from hell.

I could not bring myself to visit or call Ali's Italian landlord after my visit to New York. My resentment toward them for not being sensitive enough to understand honeymoon couples' need to be alone was over whelming. They knew it was the last time I would see Ali for over six months and yet they still sent Ali to their relative's home. Months later, before I left for Pakistan, I finally visited them at their home in Carbondale. They were quite irritated with me for waiting so long to come over. We had a stiff, uncomfortable meeting, and as I left their home I knew it would be the last time I would ever see them again.

They never realized how I blamed them for the unhappy beginning of our marriage. I suppose I was placing the blame on the wrong shoulders, but Ali was culturally bound to visit these people's relatives whom he had lived with during his time in Carbondale. Maybe he was hoping they would offer us a room at their home that night to save him the cost of a hotel room. That would have been the hospitable thing to do in Pakistan, but this was not Pakistan. Thank heaven they had no room to offer us and that possibility never materialized.

From August 1968 through December I worked very hard to earn and save money for my trip to Pakistan. I changed jobs from the university library to the university Post Office so that I was able to get more hours of work and therefore more money. I never went out with friends and lived at home with my parents saving all the money I could get my hands on. Ali wrote letters to me and gave me an address to send boxes to in Pakistan. This allowed me to have more supplies that might not be available in Pakistan or too expensive to afford because they were imported from America.

One of the important things included in these packages was approximately 20 small boxes of tampons. I doubted that I would be able to find this necessary feminine hygiene product in the other side of the world. I also sent reel-to-reel tapes of country western music and show tunes. Ali had purchased a tape recorder in Europe and brought it to Lahore. I remember one of my favorites was a Glen Campbell tape. Glen Campbell ended up keeping me company many times when I missed America. There were afternoons when I played this tape over and over again during times when I felt unhappy or frustrated with the restrictive culture. You never realize how small things such as familiar songs and voices keep you from falling into despair.

Now that I was a married woman I visited the University Medical Center and got a prescription for birth control pills. I was able to get at least six months supply and was assured that I could find more at pharmacies in Pakistan. I had no intention of getting pregnant and having a baby in a primitive country without my family around. In those days one needed to get many vaccinations for diseases we aren't exposed to here in America. I received injections for Typhoid, DPT, Tetanus, Yellow Fever, Cholera, Plague, and Small Pox during the fall of 1968. One of my best purchases was an encyclopedia of diseases and symptoms from the local, book store. I sent it to Ali in one of my supply boxes. This purchase was to prove beneficial later in my life in Pakistan.

In August of 1968 the Democratic convention was held in Chicago. Martin Luther King and Robert Kennedy had both been assassinated several months before in the spring of 1968. America was in political chaos by the time of the Democratic convention. The riots, the debates, and the candidates sparked a feeling of a new world coming to America. I watched all of the convention avidly and was most impressed with the Gore Vidal and William F. Buckley debate and fist fight on television. Eugene McCarthy, a Democratic candidate for president, was my hero and I considered him an intelligent candidate. Hubert H. Humphrey won the Democratic Party nomination on the first ballot. The war in Viet Nam was becoming a major political issue. The war was a mystery to me, but I was beginning to see that "people" were being killed on the other side of the world. I thought Gore Vidal was terrific and Buckley a war monger with only hatred on his mind in blind support of the war in Viet Nam. Of course, on November 5, 1968, Richard Nixon was elected President of the United States.

I changed my name to Lara Sayeed at the court house and at the University bursar's office. Slowly I prepared for the trip to Pakistan, got a passport in my new name, applied for a visa, and purchased my one way ticket to Karachi. Boxes of supplies were mailed to Ali while my mother and I purchased some lengths of cloth as presents for his female relatives. Soon it was time to board the plane for the trip. I had never done anything this adventuresome and was scared to death. I kept my fears to myself and told my mother and father not to worry about me, that I could take care of myself. But I was secretly worried about the trip to Pakistan. In the middle of December 1968, my parents and my twin sister, Lynne, drove me to St. Louis to board the plane. The plane I had tickets on was Pan Am going from St. Louis to New York City, and there I switched to another Pan Am flight to leave the country.

CHAPTER 3: THE SECOND WEDDING

Ali was allowed to accompany me through customs, even though the officials stopped and searched my suit cases closely. Customs was located in the main room of the Karachi airport, with several long brown tables blocking the doorway that passengers entered as they came from the plane. The customs official opened my luggage and pulled out one of my boxes of tampons. He opened one and asked in a very hostile, loud voice, in Urdu, what these strange things were while holding them high in the air in front of me. In my luggage were packed about three months supply of tampons and the rest were mailed in the boxes sent to Ali several weeks prior to the trip. I was extremely confused and had no idea what to say to this irate man dressed in military clothes. Immediately turning to Ali, I told him in English what a tampon was used for by women. Ali said something in Urdu back to the customs officer in an irritated voice and, he immediately dropped the tampon and let us through customs with no further problems.

Ali hailed a taxi and went directly to our Karachi hotel. It was a much larger and more attractive building than our New York honeymoon hotel and I was finally able to relax. Bright colorful flowers were growing everywhere, and the weather was quite warm in Karachi. It was not at all like the wet, snowy weather I had left fourteen hours earlier in Missouri. We checked into the hotel, and a porter wearing a white turban carried my luggage to our room. In the hotel room there was a queen sized bed with a velvet coverlet over a mattress, a television set, and a large bathroom with marble shower and tub. The floors, walls, and ceilings were made of white shiny marble tiles. A red and blue patterned Afghan rug covered the floor in front of the bed. Boiled water was in a closed pitcher on a table near the bed. I knew not to drink water from the hotel tap and to try and get boiled water or tea to drink where ever I went in Pakistan. I was even told to brush my teeth with boiled water as long as I was living here. Severe water borne diseases could make me ill if I was not careful with my eating and drinking habits. Physicians had told me how to avoid illness when I visited the university medical center to get inoculations for the diseases that existed in Pakistan. I was supposed to only eat fruit that had a peel or rind, such as an orange or melon. If I ate food in restaurants, I needed to avoid salads that had been washed by the kitchen staff. It was safer to purchase and cook my own food so that I knew how the food had been prepared. Any food or drink that was mixed with local water was dangerous for me to use. So I was happy to see boiled, covered water by my bedside at the hotel. Pointing to the water, I asked Ali if I could trust the hotel to give us only boiled water. He assured me the water was boiled for all Europeans and Americans. We freshened up in the hotel room and then went to a restaurant at the hotel for a quick dinner. It was pleasant, and I ordered simple rice and chicken to split with Ali. You could not buy wine in this restaurant, so tea was all I had to drink. After dinner we returned to the hotel room to catch up on everything that was not put in our letters.

Ali's plan was for us to spend the night in Karachi and then immediately fly to Lahore in the morning. That evening we finally had a honeymoon in a comfortable room, and after he quickly had sex with me in the queen sized bed, he began to explain briefly how we would be married in a Muslim ceremony the next afternoon and go to our new home in the evening for a reception/party.

I had no reason to believe our wedding would be any different than any American ceremony at a city hall or in front of a judge. My estimation of the impending celebration was wrong. He had brought to Karachi the Pakistani clothes I needed to wear for the short plane flight and family meeting at the airport. I don't know how he estimated the correct size to bring me, but I am sure he had them made by a tailor in Lahore for this purpose. It turned out to be a pair of white silk baggie pants with a draw string to tighten around my waist. The cuffs of the baggie pants had multiple lines of stitching and designs sewn into them. The pants would be worn under one of my American dresses, plus adding a beautiful silk scarf lined in gold thread that should be worn over my head at all times. Over this outfit I would wear a simulated fur coat that my grandmother had purchased for me in America. The coat looked like it was made of shearling lamb fur. Although the weather was pleasant and about 65 to 70 degrees during the winter, I wore the coat because it looked as if I was wealthy and Ali wanted me to wear it. There would be more new wedding clothes after I was prepared for the ceremony.

Ali told me that I must shave my pubic hair and take a shower before I could be married by the Mullah. He also told me that his brother's wife and several other women would be there to watch me take my shower to make sure I did everything correctly. Pakistani men thought that pubic hair was dirty, and before the wedding women must "be clean".

He cautioned me not to tell any of his friends or relatives that we had been married in a Christian ceremony in my home town in America before he returned to Pakistan. I was upset that he had told so many lies about my family and background in America to all of his family and friends. I began to wonder why it was so important for me to appear to be someone other than myself and why Ali wanted to deceive all of his family, co-workers, and friends in Pakistan. He had told everyone that my father was a retired American Diplomat to Sweden and wealthy. I was warned to continue to tell this lie to everyone when asked about my parents and not mention that my father was a Dictaphone salesman.

This untruth concerning my father upset me the most. My father was a wonderful human being who had raised my sister, brother, and me with firm convictions to tell the truth, be kind to others, and work hard in life to achieve our goals. He was an extremely handsome man, physically, mentally, and spiritually, who sang with the voice of a true tenor, believed in God, and treated woman as if they were equal to men. From my father I inherited the mechanical abilities to put any machine or event together and basic common sense were his lifelong gifts to me. I loved my father more than any person on earth, and Ali was forcing me to lie about his background. The definition of true wealth I had inherited from my father was priceless, and what Ali wanted me to do was to devalue its worth to zero. This slap in the face was the worst of all cuts I took from him, and it ate at my subconscious more than any other hurt he could command in our life together.

He told me that people would ask if we slept together and made love in Karachi and I must inform them we had separate bed rooms in the hotel. Everyone thought he had finished his Ph.D. in Carbondale at the university. I was also not allowed to let anyone know this was not true, especially his fellow professors at Punjab University. I agreed to all the lies and not to embarrass him in his own country among his relatives and friends.

I had to agree because I had no way of escape from this country or his control over me. He could not explain to me why all of this deception was necessary, but I began to understand later that it was a facade he had created to make him feel more important among his countrymen and family members while he continued to manipulate me. This was one of my first real lessons in life where I realized that superficial vestments were worthless, and that true merit lies within a person and how they treat others.

The next day I dressed in the Pakistani clothes as Ali had planned and we boarded the plane for Lahore. The flight was short and arrived at 1:00 o'clock in the afternoon at Lahore Airport, a small building that had military police inside and around the perimeter. The police were at the airport because of Pakistan's hostile relations with India. Lahore was located about five miles from the border with India, and the Army was often seen in the city guarding strategic and military sites.

About fifteen men and four women, Ali's cousins, brother, his brother's wife, and friends from the university were all there to meet us. Immediately everyone started placing garlands of flowers around my neck and handing me many bouquets of yellow flowers. The flowers all seemed to be bright yellow, orange, and rust chrysanthemums and marigolds. Soon I was overloaded with these bouquets and tried to smile and thank everyone for their attention. I had my photo taken standing with several different groups of people. Of course, the women were separate from the men, and I moved from one group to the other in order to have photos taken or to meet specific people. One or two of the women would come up behind me and pet my hair very gently. I would turn suddenly when I felt the pressure of their fingers on my head and they would move away giggling and lowering their eyes to the ground. They had never seen someone with dark blond hair and blue eyes before, so I created quite an interesting show for them. These photo opportunities lasted about one hour and finally we decided we needed to get moving to our destination. Everyone then boarded various American cars and taxis and traveled to a home of one of Ali's close friends. This man had inherited wealth from his merchant father and had a home in the suburbs of Lahore. His house was where the Mullah would come and the actual marriage was to take place. In Sunni Islam, a Mullah is a scholar who is learned in the Sharia, or rules of proper religious Islamic life. They usually preside over marriages and funerals, and often will act as preachers to inform the population of Qur'an lessons they need to learn. But first I had to be bathed and dressed carefully in red and gold wedding clothes.

When we arrived at the house, all the women immediately escorted me to the back bedroom. Located in the bedroom was a gleaming white marble bathroom with a large shower. Although the shower was smooth sided with a high water faucet and plenty of hot water, I was unprepared both emotionally and physically for the ritual that followed. One of the women gestured for me to get into the shower and handed me a safety razor and a simple bar of soap. A group of six of the women wanted to supervise my shower and make sure that all of my pubic hair was shaved off. They followed me into the bathroom, all dressed up in their finest wedding clothes. Several of them wore silk "saris" and the others had on gold and bright colored silk chemises and pants with scarves over their shoulders. While they observed closely, I slowly discarded my travel clothes and shyly slipped into the shower, which was a fairly large alcove in the marble room. There were no shower curtains or glass doors on this shower, so I was exposed to all the women's direct gazes. I had never shaved my pubic hair, must less exhibited myself in front of six women to do so. I was not exactly sure of the best way to achieve the desired results. Did I need to just start at the top and move downward, praying that I did not cut something important in the process? Throughout my shower, the women all talked in Urdu and pointed at me showering. No one volunteered to help and I am not sure I would have accepted their help if they had done so. There were places between my legs that I could not get to very easily without raising my legs or bending over to look closely at what I was doing. The room was illuminated by wonderful gold covered lamps mounted on the walls. The lights shown on my naked, wet, soapy body and made me appear to be a golden color. I was very embarrassed at the way the women looked at me and discussed my situation in a language I did not understand. I learned later that they were admiring my glowing, white skin. I must have resembled a nineteen year old movie star they had seen in some of the European movies that came to Lahore. These women were all Muslim, married, and had undergone this same ritual bath with the pubic shaving activity at sometime in their lives. No unmarried woman was allowed to watch this scene in the shower. It is interesting to me that in Pakistan woman are required to shave their pubic hair, but they don't choose to shave other hair on their bodies. I often watched as pant legs would ride up on a woman's un-shaved leg or be surprised as she lifted her arms and there was a bush of curling underarm hair. Maybe their pubic hair needed to come off so that the Muslim men could get a better look at the merchandise being presented to them.

One of the women who could speak some English asked if I had been to bed with Ali the night before. I had already been coached to say that we had slept in separate rooms the previous night. Now I was lying directly to these people because of Ali's need for secrecy and control. It was distressing to me that our Christian wedding could not be announced to all the women in the room with me.

After the shower, I was dressed in a gold and red chemise or long shirt and baggie red pants called pajamas. The chemise was made of a stiff red satin material with heavy gold threads sewn into a design throughout the satin. The gold thread scratched my shoulders when I pulled it on over my head. The chemise zipped up the right side under my arm. Again I did not know how Ali has managed to guess my size, because it fit almost exactly. On my head and shoulders one of the women draped a beautiful red scarf with gold trim. As I looked in the mirror, I realized that I was a Pakistani bride with blond hair, and everyone in the room was admiring me.

Ali entered the room and said it was time for the wedding ceremony to begin. I was told that I must pick a Pakistani name to become a Muslim bride. I did not know any names and asked a few of the women to give me choices. After listing some interesting, but practically unpronounceable names, someone mentioned the name "Layla" and I immediately asked them what it meant. It was an old fashioned name and meant "night". I said the name was fine because it was pronounceable, and told them "Layla" would be my Muslim name. Ali had said to me earlier that my own name of "Lara" meant something that was synonymous with "penis" in Urdu, so that it was not good to use it in Pakistan. He might have told me that so that it would be easier for me to accept the idea of a new name, but I never found out for sure what the name "Lara" meant in Urdu. A new name was necessary for me to be converted to Islam; it was symbolic of that conversion. I began to believe that I was playing a part in a social drama that must be improvised as we went along and my compliance was necessary to entertain the audience.

Ali then led me into the next room where all the men were waiting. I was seated in a chair, and a bearded, black robed man with a turban and an open Qur'an came and asked me to recite after him. This was the Mullah, a religious leader in Islam with little education except for being able to read the Qur'an in Arabic and possibility interpret some of it. This Mullah was uneasy around me, and I noticed that he would not look me in the face, but just read from the Qur'an. Ali was there coaching me to say Urdu and Arabic words I did not know or understand. I found it odd that Ali did not interpret what the Mullah said to the audience or to me. Of course, the audience knew what was happening and understood the Arabic words, which I did not.

Later I learned that the translation of what I had said among other Arabic phrases were the following:

"There is no god but Allah
and Mohammed is his prophet."

Without knowing it, I had just been converted to Islam without understanding what had happened, and certainly without my consent. I was told by Ali to recite some other sentences, and then the ceremony was over. Once again I was married to this man from Lahore, only this time it was as a Muslim woman, and it was extremely hard to tell when it actually occurred. During the ceremony I was never asked "do you take this man" to be your husband. I believe that the men performed some ceremony in this room when I was not present and Ali was asked to sign a document saying he was taking me as a wife. Muslim women don't even need to say "yes" to be married.

During the years after the 2001 World Trade Center bombing by fanatical Muslim terrorists, I have read many different declarations about how people can convert to Islam and why it is the perfect religion for women to become involved. Several times I heard government officials say that Islam is a religion of peace. In my opinion, Islam is one of the most chauvinistic religions in the world with terrifying ideology for any woman. Living in Pakistan showed me the reality of Islamic life, day-to-day subjugation of women from birth to old age. In Islam, women are commodities and treated as such by Pakistani society, their own fathers, brothers, and husbands.

I did not sign a document concerning this Islamic marriage, so I have wondered if women have any legal authority in marriage or divorce. They just submit to their husbands' and fathers' wishes in becoming legally attached to any man who decides to marry them.

I did not know that Ali could not have easily married a Christian girl without much controversy and family trouble. To be Christian was to be considered an infidel, and while the Qur'an said it was permissible for a Muslim man to marry a Christian girl, it was necessary to convert her to Islam when the marriage happened. When he had returned from the United States to Pakistan and announced that we would be married, he told his family that I would convert without ever mentioning it to me. I said the words he instructed me to say without knowing what these words meant or realizing the reasons or prejudices behind the entire ceremony. Later I found out that Christians were treated badly in Pakistan, and to this day are discriminated against, beaten, taxed heavily, and sometimes killed without any negative action for the murders. The Qur'an has specific verses that instruct Muslim men to treat harshly anyone who has the unique opportunity to become Muslim and refuses to do so. The death penalty is easily given to anyone who has converted to Islam and then later decides to change religions again. Any Muslim who renounces Islam is condemned to die if they are in a Muslim country. The belief behind this law is that any convert persisting in deliberate rejection of the "truth" as given to Muhammad by the Angel Gabriel deserves to die. To leave Islam is not considered an option if you are born a Muslim and want to convert to Christianity, Buddhism, Judaism or any other religion in the world. You must always remain a Muslim or become an outcast and face certain death in many Islamic countries. This belief by Muslims has even followed converts to other countries and no one is safe from extremists who believe that Allah is speaking to them through this violent message in the Qur'an.

After having tea and sweet cakes it was time to board our fleet of black American and European cars or taxis and travel to the home that Ali was renting and we would be living in while in Pakistan. The house was near the university and was actually a large apartment. It was located on the second floor, up a long stair way with an iron gate at the bottom. The address was number 25 Faiz Road, Muslim Town, Lahore, Pakistan. Ali's mother was waiting in the apartment and as I entered the front door she hugged me and showered me with kisses and many prayers in Arabic. She had not come to the wedding ceremony or the preparation for the wedding. I believe she did not like to leave the house often because of her faith. She never attended school, but had somehow memorized the Qur'an and was able to recite passages perfectly. Mahji was extremely religious and tried to practice the five pillars of Islam. She seemed to have some common sense and was not one of the flighty, delicate, air headed women I would meet during my stay. Mahji had been through many hardships in her life and survived them all. No one had any idea how old she really was, but I estimate around 75 years old in 1968. That would mean that she was born around 1893 in India and probably first married in about 1908. Girls were married quite young in India and Mahji had nice facial features and cheek bones. She was probably a pretty young girl when she was married. Several of her children had died in infancy and Ali's older brother, Salim was the first child to live to adulthood. Salim was approximately fifty-five years old at this time and working for the government of Pakistan.

Family members streamed into the house along with friends and university personnel. Copper trays of various sweet cakes and steaming pots of tea in very large silver pots were available to everyone, while Pakistani music was playing in the background on a tape recorder. The women immediately separated from the men and went to the back bedroom. I was quickly hustled into the bedroom and seated on a large bed covered with a velvet quilt. There the women would come close to me, stare, and try out their limited English vocabulary. The other women sat directly on the floor or on a few short stools around the room. The room was crowded and noisy, and I became irritated with the women's constant Urdu chattering. I was offered sweet cakes, candy, and sugared ginger, but after tasting one of them I could eat no more because they were extremely saccharine. The walls of the bedroom were painted a light blue color and the floor was concrete. There was a multi-colored cotton carpet on this floor, and I noticed that high on one of the walls near the ceiling a gecko lizard was trying to hide. A set of French doors were located at the far end of the room and opened out on a small, walled balcony which overlooked the neighbor's court yard.

One of the women confided to me that Ali had the bed built especially for me. It was a fairly large bed, about queen sized, with a head board painted in flowers and bright colors. The mattress was a type of Pakistani futon, cotton stuffed, hard, and about two inches thick. It was covered in a heavy gray cotton cloth. The sheets were, of course, cotton, white, and embroidered with flowers. The sheets rubbed my delicate skin raw until after they had been washed about fifty times. The bed was painted in gaudy colors, but as I lived longer in Lahore I realized it was done in a subdued style compared to other furniture made in the city. Ali had also purchased a dressing table with mirror and small padded seat. Drawers on the sides of the dressing table allowed me to put make-up, hair brush, etc. out of reach of the small children, such as Ali's many nephews.

Soon Ali came into the room and presented me with beautiful 22 karat gold jewelry. There were eight 22 karat gold carved bracelets, two very heavy 22 karat gold earrings with carvings on the length of the circles. I received a gold ring with a large ruby in the center and another gold ring with a white/clear stone which could have been a large diamond, but roughly cut. There was also a 22 karat gold necklace with a red inlay of some type - I believe the inlay on the necklace was enamel - which Ali draped around my neck. Brides are supposed to wear all the jewelry at once, appearing over dressed, but in correct Pakistani fashion.

By this time I was getting hungry and thirsty because I had not been offered any food except the overly sweet cakes. I knew not to drink the water without boiling it, so I insisted upon tea as a beverage. I told Ali I was starving and could he find some food for me to eat. He went to the other room and prepared a plate, but the food was so spicy hot and filled with curry that it was inedible for me. However, seeing my predicament, Mahji finally produced some plain rice with lentils and some yogurt. This small dinner filled me up for the evening so I did not faint from hunger. It had been at least eight hours since a breakfast of two eggs and toast in Karachi.

So much was happening around me, music, people talking, comings and goings from the room, photos being taken, that I had sensory and mental overload and could not think clearly. Ali was mostly in the other room with the men guests, resulting in my inability to get information on what was happening or the meaning of different sentences spoken to me. He had not really prepared me for this atmosphere and I was extremely confused and tired by this time of day. In 1968 no one knew much about jet lag, but I am sure I must have been experiencing it these first few days in Lahore.

Through all of this activity and celebration Mahji sat quietly on a rug about 15 feet from the bed, saying her Muslim prayer beads. Her mouth was always moving in silent prayer as she slowly counted her beads. It was similar to a rosary that a Catholic might use, but with 99 beads instead of 59. Mahji had hers constantly with her and in any spare moment would start praying. The other women totally ignored her and chatted with each other while they stared and pointed at me. A rosary in Pakistan is called a

"Mala" and can refer to anything strung like beads or even a garland of flowers.

I needed to use the toilet and had no idea where it was located or even if we had one. I asked one of the older children to go out into the other room and get Ali for me. They only understood that I was calling for Ali, because of my inability to speak Urdu. So a young child ran into the living room and promptly returned with my husband.

Bathrooms in Pakistan are something quite different from American bathrooms. Just finding the toilet would be interesting, especially when a party was in full swing. The men were in the living room and dining room playing music and eating. All the women were segregated to the back bedroom. There were two bathrooms were located on the staircase leading up to the apartment. One was just a toilet and sink while the other included a shower with these fixtures. The toilet consisted of two concrete foot pads with a hole in the floor between them. The hole for the toilet was also made of polished concrete and about the size and shape of a large melon. The toilets flushed when you pulled a chain and sent the sewage into a pipe that flowed into a canal outside the house. Ali escorted me through the back bedroom, then through the kitchen and out the front door to avoid the men in the living room area. On the landing at the top of the stairs he opened one of the bathroom doors and proceeded to explain to me the way to use the toilet. After he left the room and I had locked the door, I tried to balance over the hole in the floor to urinate. Luckily the wall was close by and I could hold on to it with one hand. You were supposed to squat and place each foot on the foot pads. There was no toilet paper, only a filled jug with a spout for pouring water over your groin area to clean it. It took me a few tries to be able to balance over the hole in the floor, but it worked out, and over time I finally got pretty good at it. The experience gives you great calf and thigh muscles over extended periods of time.

Many eastern countries believe the American's use of toilet paper is a dirty practice. Everyone in the family uses the same jug for the bathroom, and there is no soap or towels for cleaning your hands afterwards. You are supposed to pour the water from the jug with your right hand, while directing the water flow and wipe your groin with your left hand. This is the reason for the practice in Muslim countries of only eating food with their right hand. Many people in Pakistan eat only with their hands using bread to scoop up the food and do not use forks or spoons. The next day I made sure that both bathrooms were supplied with soap bars, towels and cleaning supplies. Ali waited outside the bathroom door and escorted me back to the bedroom when I had finished. The less I was seen by the Muslim men in the living room, the better. It is not considered proper for men other than your husband and family members to see a new bride or any woman who was not their sister, mother, or wife.

Finally the party was over, people went home and allowed us to relax, get undressed, and go to bed. We were left alone to talk about the day and evening guests at the party. Ali explained a few of the traditions, but was not much of a talker that evening. I was tired from the trip, but we had sex that night in our new bed and I slept marginally well; at least I was finally in Pakistan safe with my husband. Ali certainly appreciated the new bare coiffeur located between my legs. Sex with Ali was less than satisfactory. Most Muslim men are raised to believe that women should not enjoy sex, and in some Islamic countries women's genitals are mutilated to stop them from having any sexual climax. When we were in bed together he would immediately start playing with his penis and, when sufficiently erect, roll over on me and try to insert it. Even though young and passionate, I needed a little more foreplay than his brief prelude to paradise. After being in Pakistan for over three months I would wait for Ali to be asleep and start masturbating myself to an orgasm. He slept so soundly that he never heard any of my urgent self-help sessions on the other side of the bed. He never tried to hug or kiss me during the day or even hold hands because any public contact between men and women was frowned upon in Pakistan. His mother and nephews were always around the house so that I never had any privacy except in the bathrooms. If I initiated a hug or touching of any kind, Ali immediately thought I wanted to have sex with him and he would pull me down on the bed. These encounters were quite brief, and after he got started he would orgasm within two minutes. I was left barely beginning to heat up and extremely frustrated. If I mentioned to him that his love making was rather abrupt, he just replied that I was so sexy he could not help himself. So there was no such thing as a romantic evening out or even an evening alone at home with wine and dinner. All of my notions concerning romance or love making were not happening for me while Ali obliviously went through his day and evening believing all was perfectly fine. Why shouldn't he feel that way about sex? Men are not taught how to treat women lovingly in Islamic countries because women are considered inferior to men. Women only exist to give men pleasure, not the other way around.

I began to realize that there was a huge amount of information, traditions, and language to try and learn during the days to come. In the beginning I didn't see what was happening to me or believe that these small lies and compromises were changing me. I rationalized all these things by saying to myself that Ali's friends and relatives would never meet my family. I would be leaving Pakistan in less than two years and probably never see these people again. If it was important for Ali to put a different spin on who I was and where my parents came from, this was a way for him to achieve status in his culture. I would be a good wife; I wanted to fit in and please Ali, so I did what I was told. I had no power in this country and was totally at the mercy of Ali and his family. Over the years I realized that lying was a cultural norm in Pakistan. Telling a lie doesn't mean the same thing as in American culture. Status, how one appears, is much more important than telling the truth in Islam. Slowly I submerged my own American, Midwestern beliefs and ideals to keep my husband and everyone else happy. But these compromises slowly ate away at my self esteem.

I begin pushing everything I believed to be important deep into a secret place in my head. Eventually, all I had been taught growing up came roaring back into my consciousness, and I began to despise the people who asked me to lie to the world about myself. But this would not happen for many more years after my life in Pakistan.

The next day I got out of bed late and ran to the bathroom on the landing, only this time through the living room and not the back bedroom. No one was in the house except Ali, Mahji, and a young man named Babur. After the bathroom trip I went to the kitchen looking for something to eat. Mahji was already up and busy in the kitchen cooking and cleaning up from the wedding party the night before. Ali was having tea in the living room, relaxing as if he were the master of the house, which, of course, he was supposed to be. Everyone greeted me by the traditional "A Salaam Al Akum" (Go with God). I learned to say immediately "Wow Akum Salaam" (You go with God, too), the proper answer. Mahji spoke no English and I spoke no Urdu, so communications were difficult between us. I was asked what I wanted to eat for breakfast. Ali translated and I answered that two boiled eggs would be fine for breakfast. I asked about toast, too, but no one had any loaves of bread in slices or plastic packages. Mahji quickly made flat bread, called roti, very much like a tortilla, and cooked it on a metal plate over the burner of the stove. It was delicious, and I was happy to have something without spices or pepper.

I immediately began learning a few Urdu words, mainly based around food items and social greetings. Mahji would ask me what I wanted for lunch or dinner, so she could send a man or boy to pick it up in the market place. I learned how to say my favorite food items over time, and she would cook the dishes for me. She taught me pronunciation of some of the words, laughing when I said them incorrectly, although she generally left this job to Ali or Babur. Often Mahji would make two sets of food for dinner, one with heavy spices and one without. This was a courtesy to me because I could rarely eat the hot pepper, curry, or spices that were used constantly in the Pakistani food dishes. Rice and lamb, spinach mixed with lamb, lentil cakes, chicken, rice, goat meat, and Chai tea were some of my favorite foods. Yogurt was at every meal, and we made our own daily from a culture and some boiled whole milk. I enjoyed varieties of rice, too, white long grain usually. Brown rice was considered sub-standard and only for poor people to eat. Saffron rice with lentils or peas was served often at our table. Most of these dishes had lots of mild spice, but without pepper.

Mahji rarely went shopping for any type of food product. She would send a man or older boy out to purchase food for the household. That first morning in Lahore, I met Ali's oldest nephew, Babur. Ali's brother Salim had eleven children – ten sons and one daughter. Babur, the oldest son, was about sixteen and nice looking. He had taken some English classes and could speak broken sentences to me. It was a great relief to have another person in the house that could talk to me and explain local customs when I had questions. Salim had married his first cousin and had started having children about 17 years ago. He named all of his sons after the Moghul Emperors of India. Their names were Babur, Sikandar, Ibrahim, Jahangir, Akbar, Hakim, Parwez, Aurangzeb, Sher Shah, and Khurram. There was one little girl approximately ten or eleven years old named Fozia. She was a beautiful girl and appeared to be smart, but all of the boys treated her roughly and teased her often. She was forced to work around her mother's house and did not attend school past a few early grades when she was younger. Her job as the daughter was to help her mother with house work and cooking until she was old enough to be married and go to another man's household. She could be married any time from aged 13 years to about 21 years old, depending upon when her father found a suitable husband for her. Arranged marriages with the girl older than 21 years would label the girl as an old maid with something possibly wrong in her family.

Girls got married at a young age in Pakistan if their fathers decided to make the match for them. Both poor people and rich people arranged the marriages of their daughters, often with their first cousins. The marriages were almost always arranged by their fathers, and usually the girls had absolutely no say in who they married. The Qur'an supposedly gives women the right to reject any man they do not wish to marry, but in reality very few women are ever consulted. Their fathers have the only authority to accept or reject a marriage offer for the daughter. If the father is dead, the oldest brother has complete control over his sister's life and must give consent for her to marry. Marriage is very important to all women because they are not allowed to have homes of their own without being married. A single woman living alone or with friends is not allowed in this male dominated society. If found to be unguarded or living alone women, will be raped or worse by gangs of young men. Even widows live with either their husbands family or go home to live with their own family after the death of their husband.

I had the opportunity to walk through the rest of the apartment about noon that day. It was large and the rooms had high ceilings. We were probably renting over 1,800 square feet in this apartment. Our living areas were on the second floor, with a winding stair case leading up from the iron gate at the street. There was a second winding staircase off the porch and going up to the roof. Two bathrooms were located off the staircase leading up to a landing or small porch. Inside the screen door from the landing was a breakfast or dining room and a small kitchen. The new refrigerator Ali purchased in Europe with his gambling money was up against the wall in the breakfast room. The floor and walls were all made of concrete painted a light gray color. There were no pictures or paintings decorating any of the walls. A dining table with six chairs stood in the middle of the room. This table was made out of wood with a dull yellow colored Formica top. The kitchen was adjacent to the breakfast room and was much smaller in size with a tiny, square, high window. There was only a water faucet coming out of the wall and a drain in the floor in this kitchen. No cabinets or shelves were built into the walls as would have been in an American kitchen. Mahji cooked on a small two burner gas stove which resembled something we would take camping in America. This stove sat directly on the floor with a stool next to it. When Mahji cooked she sat on the stool and had multiple iron cooking pots surrounding her. She would put them on the stove at various times to get the food exactly as she liked it. Vegetables and fruit would also lie on the floor within reach of her hand and knives. Sometimes you would see onions or garlic hanging from hooks on the wall, and often there were other vegetables native to Pakistan that I was not familiar with hanging there.

Behind the kitchen was a small bedroom with a twin sized "char pi" bed. The word "char" means four, so this bed was called "four legs". These beds are made out of four wooden legs and a frame with rope stretched across the frame in a strong netting. The rope is woven in a pattern which allows it to hold one or even two people about twenty-four inches off the ground. These beds were light in weight and could be easily moved around the house. We had about four of them in various rooms for Mahji and nephews to spend the night as needed. People slept or lounged on char pi-like day beds in America. There was a cotton stuffed mattress, much like a futon, covering the rope netting.

The only other thing in the room was Mahji's prayer rug. A small wool pile rug woven mostly in red and black threads, it was just large enough for her to kneel upon five times per day. She also owned a large, old Qur'an that was kept wrapped in red velvet cloth when not in use. Mahji's adherence to Islam was complete. She observed the five pillars of Islam, which are confession of the faith, daily prayer, alms giving, fasting during Ramadan, and the Pilgrimage to Mecca. Her one regret was that she had not been able to take the "Haj", or pilgrimage, to Mecca yet, because she could not afford to pay for it. Her two sons had promised to send her to Mecca on Haj someday soon.

The second staircase outside continued to wind upward to a flat roof. On the way to the roof was another small bedroom. It was empty except for a few gecko lizards on the wall and ceiling. The walls and stairs were concrete painted a light gray in most places and chipping paint in others. The roof was a multi-purpose room. It was strong enough to hold many people walking or sleeping on it. A four foot high wall entirely surrounded the roof top. Most roof tops in Pakistan are used for sleeping in the hot weather and just relaxing or looking at the view other parts of the year. Mahji would hang our washed clothes on the roof to dry throughout the year. We did not have a clothes washer or dryer for the house, so we either washed it by hand or sent it to the cleaners. I asked several times if the cleaners were anything like what we had in America, but never got much of a comparison from Ali.

The view from the house top was magnificent. I could see a lot of the city of Lahore and countryside from various vantage points. Walking on the roof was a safe and private way to pass the time. Sometimes I took a char pi (bed) up to the roof so I could lounge and read books. When Mahji was cleaning the house, I usually retreated to the roof just to get away from her. She would not allow me to help her with any chores.

One day as I was on the roof watching village life below me in the street I noticed a young woman following a water buffalo. As the water buffalo defecated large chunks of dung, the woman would immediately pick the steaming dung up in her bare hands, shape it into a flat pie, and stack it in her "rumal" or large cloth tied around her neck like a sling. She would later take the 20 or 30 dung patties back to her hut and slap them up on an outside wall or put it flat on the ground to dry in the sun. When dried, these dung patties made an excellent fuel for the cooking fire. Many people saved dung patties and used them for fuel. You could also buy ten of them on the street for one Ana, or less than a penny. Dried dung patties are considered a "lower class" fuel used only by the poor. People with any money use white gas or charcoal for their cooking fires.

After having observed this woman, the dung collector, I always watched for buildings with buffalo dung plastered along their walls to dry. I began to notice more and more people using this fuel for their road side cooking fires. I thought it was a good use of natural resources and served two purposes. It kept the city streets clean, and heated homes and cooking fires for the poor.

CHAPTER 4: TENTH OF MUHJARRAM

Ali and his family were Sunni Muslims, which are somewhat more liberal minded than the extremist Shiite Muslims. Ali had a close boyhood friend who was a Shia. This Shiite man had known Ali as a child and played with him in the dark, dirty streets of the old walled city. He attended our wedding and was a guest in our home many times. I met him personally several days after arriving in Lahore and after the wedding. His name was Shahji and he could speak excellent English. He was shorter than me, and quite slender in build. I never heard a harsh word from him or a complaint of any kind. He also enjoyed visiting us and ignored my stubborn decision not to be veiled or wear the burkah as his women relatives did whenever they went out in public. He was not married and lived with his older brother, mother, sister, brother's wife and two children in a small house about two miles from our apartment. Shahji had a government job as a clerk somewhere in Lahore. He drove a small Japanese motorcycle to get around town and to his job every day. Shahji was not highly educated, no advanced degrees like my husband Ali, but seemed intelligent, with common sense and wit. He always had a joke or story to tell us and laugh about when he visited. I enjoyed his company and conversation often when he came to see his friend, Ali.

The term Shia is a shortened form of "Shiat Ali", which means "the party of Ali". The Imam Ali was the Prophet Muhammad's adoptive brother, but he was also his son-in-law having married Fatima, the Prophet's favorite daughter. The Prophet Muhammad did not have any sons during his lifetime – only daughters, so his sons-in-law became extremely important in the history of Islam. Caliph Ali and Fatima produced several grandsons for Muhammad and they grew up to be prominent men. This was over 1300 years ago and the influence of this desert family is still being felt on modern day Shiites and the Western World. Unfortunately, Mohammed's son-in-law, Ali, died in 661 AD and there seemed to be some disagreement among the population of Arabia and Iraq over who should inherit the "Caliphate" after his death. A Caliph is the guardian of Islamic law and the Islamic State. Ali, Muhammad's son-in-law, had two sons with his wife Fatima. Their names were Hasan and Husain, and they were the Prophet Muhammad's grandsons. Despite this important lineage and relationship to Muhammad, neither grandson inherited the coveted ruling position of Caliph and it passed instead to another dynasty in what is now Iraq. Of course, this situation caused some dissent and opposition to the Iraqi rulers from strict Muslims. Those who believed that the rightful heirs of Muhammad should be in control were known as Shiites. For them the heir to the Caliphate would be the "Mahdi", a leader guided personally and directly by God. So this situation led to a military battle at Karbala in 680 AD. Karbala is located in Iraq, not too far from Baghdad. Karbala is the holy Muslim city that was in the news so often in 2004 because of extremist Shiites and a local Imam fighting the American army.

In the famous battle Ali's son Husain and his many followers were completely massacred by the opposing army. Husain is treated much like a Christ figure in Shia Islam. Every year penitential processions of young men occur in Lahore and other Muslim cities on the anniversary of the death of Husain. This particular anniversary is a very holy day, celebrated on the tenth of Muhjarram on the Muslim calendar. The Muslim calendar is based on the cycles of the new moon, so the date changes each year. But it corresponds generally to about the middle of January on our western calendar.

Ritual mourning for Imam Husain is performed on this day by groups of young men. Shia women usually stay at home and mourn the death with wailing and crying. My husband, Ali, thought it might be interesting for me to observe the Lahore procession and the ritual mourning of the local Shiite population and I agreed with him. Watching this procession of fanatical Shiites would be interesting for me to observe. The problem was how to watch it and remain safe while surrounded by thousands of Shiites in ritual mourning frenzies. About 77% of the population of Pakistan is Sunni and 20% are Shia. The remaining 3% of the Lahore population is a mixture of Christians and Parsee.

Safety was a big issue during this particular holiday. Most Sunni Muslims thought that the ritual mourning got a little violent and extreme every year. The Shiites were psychologically overwhelmed in the mourning activities for Imam Husain, who had died over 1300 years ago in the Iraqi desert. Women wailed and cried as if their fathers or sons had recently been slaughtered. Men beat themselves repeatedly with their fists in a rhythmic cadence of blows to their chest. This chest beating went on for hours and often caused heavy bruising or bleeding. Some men would make a cat-o-nine tails fashioned out of chains with small knives at the end of each chain. They would then whip themselves with these knives while crying louder and louder "Imam Husain, Imam Husain" repeatedly. The cry is taken up by everyone who is Shiite and the religious frenzy it creates lasts the entire day. Only the Shiites mourned the death of Imam Husain, so the Sunnis could watch from the sidelines in houses, behind windows, or on the sides of streets lining the way. A huge procession formed and wound through the city slowly during the day and ended up at a Shiite mosque in the Old City of Lahore.

Ali thought that if I dressed conservatively, covering my blond hair with a dark shawl, we could go down to the old city and watch from the street. As body guards he enlisted the aid of four strapping males, all his cousins, who were tall, tough, Punjabi men. We gathered with the cousins early in the day at our apartment and went by car as close as we dared to Lahore's old walled city. The traffic was heavy but we parked near enough to walk the rest of the way through the teaming streets to where the procession would be passing in front of us. Surrounding me the entire time these four Punjabi men seemed nervous. Ali stayed at my side and tried to explain to me in a low voice what was happening in the procession. Keeping as quiet as possible during our walk was difficult for me but I did not point or gesture at anything for fear of being noticed by the Shiites. As we moved down the street we saw many young men with blood stained T-shirts and pants where their own fists had broken the skin and blood dripped all the way down their trousers. These men would beat themselves for hours to show that they were properly grieving for Imam Husain. A Shiite man who did not have marks on his body from this holy day would be considered unobservant. Watching the mob of Sunnis carefully surrounding the Shiite procession, we moved along with the flow of people. What I saw was frightening to me. It was hard to believe that these thousands of men could be in such a religious frenzy they would harm themselves, sometimes fatally, in memory of an Imam who had been dead for 1300 years. The procession was led by a high level Mullah, dressed in black and walking in front of the thousands of young men, leading a riderless, pure white Arabian horse. It might have been historically correct that Imam Husain rode a pure white Arabian horse, but I got the distinct impression that it was there for the effect it created on the crowd. The particular cleric leading the horse was fairly young, about 35, and carried a young boy on his shoulders. The boy was also totally dressed in black and seemed frightened by the noise and large crowd. This horse signified Imam Husain's martyrdom at the battle of Karbala. Everyone near the horse was dressed in black, wearing turbans and flowing robes. These men were leaders of the local Shiite congregation, all members of one family and important in the Shia community of Lahore. Supposedly they all were related by blood in some distant way to a 9th century Caliph. The procession consisted of men walking and riding on flat bed trucks, each one with blood dripping down his bare back or white t-shirt, after having beaten himself steadily with either knives or other instruments of torture. As I watched the men in white T-shirts I realized how well the red blood stains were accentuated for the crowd. White is a good background color for red blood which soon turns to black. It was almost as if the men were vain about their bleeding bodies and wanted to make sure their efforts were appreciated by others in the crowd. The wailing and crying was everywhere and "Imam Husain" was repeated over and over again by the faithful. The scene was amazing to watch as it wound through the streets of Lahore.

Sunni Muslims watched from the sidewalks and lined the cobblestone street. If any one of them had said or done something against Shias or the leaders of the procession, they would have been mobbed by thousands of believers and dragged from the sidelines to be badly beaten or killed. The procession resembled a black and red snake moving slowly through the tan colored dirt and cobblestone streets. You could see the blood on the road side and running off the flat bed trucks as the men bled themselves for their sacred Imam.

This was my first experience with religious fanatics and it made a big impression on me. The next day, we visited the home of Ali's friend Shahji, a Shiite, and talked about what I had seen during the procession. Shahji was walking somewhere in the middle of the thousands of young men, but he was only beating his chest. He knew he had to work the days afterward and could not afford to hurt himself too significantly during this holiday. Ali asked Shahji to lift his shirt up and we all cringed at his bright red and bruised chest. We inquired if his wounds pained him and he said that it only troubled him a little bit when he slept. Every year he carefully showed his devotion by participating in the procession, beating his chest, and issuing forth many "Imam Husain" yells, but immediately afterwards returned to his normal life style.

My husband, Ali, had never seen the faces of his best friend's sister or brother's wife. The women in a Shiite home were kept in the back room and away from men who were not members of their family. Shahji asked me to visit them separately in the back room and have tea with them. I responded that I would be happy to go into the back room for a few minutes to say hello, but had no intention of drinking tea there and that I expected to be served with the men in the living room. No one wanted to argue about my decision, so the men just shrugged and turned right into the living room to talk in Urdu. I turned left into another small room where four women and some infant children were all seated on carpets on the floor. The room was only lit with a few small lamps but, while dark, I was able to observe the four women. The women were dressed in brightly colored outfits and all had scarves tied over their head as good Muslim women. They giggled when I entered the room and gestured for me to sit on a single chair that they had brought into the room. I greeted them with the traditional "Salaam al Akum" (go with God) but that was the only phrase I had learned so far during my stay. All of the women had long, black hair that was styled in one long braid down their backs to their waists. They braided brightly colored ribbons in and out of their braids and tied it in a knot at the bottom to secure their hair. It was obvious to me that these women were Shahji's unmarried sister, his mother, and his brother's wife. The young children looked like a boy and girl, with their hair shaved very short and earrings in the girl's pierced ears.

None of the women spoke English, mainly because they were not allowed to go to school past sixth grade. Smiling, I sat down with them for only a few minutes, while they chattered and looked me over. The children came over to touch my hair and look closely at me. In a few minutes boredom overcame my good manners and I decided suddenly it was tea time. I smiled and got up from my chair, leaving the room and moving into the living room with the men.

This living room was furnished a little better than the room I had just left, with two sofas, covered in flowered upholstery, and totally swathed in clear plastic to protect them from harm. A small coffee table was in front of the sofas and a floor lamp was situated between them. I sat down with the three men in the room and greeted Shahji's older brother with a smile. I never had a problem looking men directly in the face but it always seemed to make many Muslim men nervous. Shahji's father had died many years ago, so his older brother was considered the head of the family. This was his house and his wife and children who lived with him. His mother also resided here and helped watch the children and clean house. In America the widow would have inherited the home when her husband died, but not in Pakistan. The oldest son of this family, and many others in Pakistan, have more legal precedence than a father's widow.

Shahji's sister was also one of the women living in the house. She was unmarried and it was the responsibility of the elder brother to find a proper husband for her soon. She would then leave the house for her husband's family home after the wedding. There were no prospects at this time that anyone told me about, so the girl was getting older fast and might be considered an old maid in a few years.

I turned, smiled, and sweetly asked everyone in the room if the elder brother's wife would like to join us for tea in the living room. I believe I made them all uncomfortable with my inquiry. According to some Islamic scholars there is nothing in the Qur'an which requires a degree of segregation, veiling of all women, or their seclusion in a separate part of a man's house. This did not seem to matter or be followed by the Pakistani Shiites, and their women were always kept as far away from outside men as possible. Shahji's brother announced that his wife and mother would feel more comfortable staying right where they were in the back room of the house. When the tea was ready one of the women brought it to a curtain separating the kitchen from the living room. She called out in a soft voice and Shahji went over to the curtain and picked up the tray that was left for him. The tray had a tea pot, covered with a "tea cozy", a cream pitcher, several cups and saucers, and some sweet cakes. They had obviously expected us to visit and gotten some special desserts at the bakery earlier in the day. Most Pakistanis served tea with cream and no one cared or asked if I preferred lemon. Sugar was usually a large grained, rough, natural type of sugar. Fine grained sugar or sugar cubes were expensive and generally only served in hotels or restaurants.

After an hour or so of sipping tea and eating cakes, Ali and I said goodbye and hailed a taxi to take us back to our own house. The taxis were everywhere on the street and you could always count on getting one easily no matter what time of the day or night you needed it. The cars were usually black in color, made in Britain, and several years old. Taxis would take you anywhere you wanted to go and they were often driven exceedingly fast. I wondered if we would arrive at our destination alive when in a taxi. There were several other modes of transportation available, such as rickshaws pulled either by horse or human. Most of these rickshaws were found nearer to the old walled city rather than out here in the suburbs, but occasionally you could find one near our apartment. The rickshaws were cheaper and open to the night air, but the taxis could go faster and were only slightly more comfortable to ride in when you were going a far distance.

The Qur'an is said to have been revealed to Muhammad in Arabic, of course; that is the only language that Muhammad spoke. It is considered the highest authority in Islam because it is believed to have been dictated by Allah and delivered to the Prophet Muhammad by the Angel Gabriel. However, the Prophet Muhammad was not a scholar and could not even write Arabic, so he dictated the revelations to several scribes or secretaries over a long period of time. In 622 AD he founded the first Islamic state, the theocracy in Medina, a city in western Saudi Arabia located north of Mecca. Two branches of the Islamic religion developed over time, Shiite and Sunni. The Sunni branch believes that the first four Caliphs - Muhammad's successors - rightly took his place as the leaders of Islam. Sunni's recognize the heirs of the four Caliphs as legitimate religious leaders. These heirs ruled continuously in the Muslim world until the break-up of the Ottoman Empire following the end of the First World War. The last Caliph left Istanbul, Turkey to be exiled to Switzerland until he died as an old man.

Shiites, in contrast, believe that only the heirs of the fourth Caliph, Ali, are the legitimate successors of Muhammad. Shia Muslims also revere Ali as the first Imam, and his descendants, beginning with his sons Hasan and Husain, continue the line of the Imams until the twelfth. The Shia Muslims believe that the twelfth Imam disappeared in 939 AD. Allah will command him to manifest again on this earth as the Mahdi when he is needed. So everyone in the Islamic world is still waiting for the Mahdi to show up. Shiite Muslims have another rather distinct emphasis, which is their visitation to religious shines dedicated to various religious leaders. In Iraq, these shrines include the tomb of the Caliph Ali in Najaf and that of his son, Imam Husain, in Karbala. Both of the extremely important shrines and their surrounding towns have been attacked by American troops in the Iraqi war. Shiite Muslims all over the world are offended about this desecration of their holy places and they will never forgive America for what they consider a great blasphemy to their holiest places. The worst possible nightmare that could easily happen would be for a stray American missile to accidentally disinter Caliph Ali or the Imam Husain from their final resting place. Then the Western world would really begin to see a Jihad, or holy war, against all involved in the Iraq war.

Ali informed me after were arrived home that, as a new American citizen in Lahore, I must register with the American Embassy. It seems that embassy personnel always keep records on where America's various citizens were located in Pakistan just in case they needed to evacuate. This seemed like a good idea, so the next morning we took a taxi to the American consulate, showed them my passport, and filled out a form. It was legal for me to stay in Pakistan now, and if there was any trouble in Lahore I would be notified by my own government.

CHAPTER 5: THE UGLY AMERICANS

One morning in early February 1969 the door bell rang unexpectedly at our Lahore apartment. One of Ali's nephews staying with us went to find out who was at the door. He ran down the gray concrete steps and returned in two minutes with a sealed white envelope in his hand. The gold embossed seal of the United States of America was in the upper left corner and my name was hand written on the center front of the envelope in a flowing script. As I nervously opened it, I wondered what this could possibly mean, for I was not acquainted with any Americans in Lahore and did not know why the Consul would be sending me a note. Ali, his mother and the nephews were gathered around me and watched me open the envelope tentatively. Inside there was an invitation, hand written, to a tea party at the home of the American Consul. The invitation was on a gold trimmed white paper and delicately signed by the wife of the Consul General. Everyone in the room was impressed with what appeared to be a validation of my status at the American Consulate. This invitation, no doubt, backed-up Ali's lie that I was the daughter of a diplomat. I was nervous and could not figure out why a 20 year old girl from Carbondale, Illinois would be invited to a tea party by the wife of the Consul General of West Pakistan. Maybe all of the new Americans were invited every month or so to this type of welcoming party? The entire family group discussed the invitation and it was soon decided that we must go and purchase new clothes so that I could dress appropriately for the event. The date of the tea party was approximately two weeks away. We would have to find some fine material and have a tailor make a chemise and pajama (pants) outfit for me. A short trip down into Lahore's walled old city shopping district to obtain the cloth was the only place Ali knew to find quality cloth and have something made for me. It never crossed my mind that I would wear anything but a Pakistani outfit, even though I had brought American styled dresses with me. In Pakistan all American women's clothes were too risqué to be worn out in public by Pakistani women.

Later in the day we took a taxi down to the historic walled city and walked to a shopping district inside the imposing Bhati Gate. The great wall around the city had four large gates built into the adobe like hard mud bricks which was the construction material used hundreds of years ago. This wall surrounded the old city and all the gates are extremely impressive with inlaid marble and imposing columns.

Some of the districts inside each gate are famous for the particular occupations of the residents in that area. Inside the Roshnai Gate is the famous "red light" district filled with small bedroom storefronts that men will walk down to view the women they might want to rent for the night or only a few minutes. Each woman, if she is not occupied, stands in the doorway displaying herself as only a Muslim prostitute can possibly be clothed. Very heavy make-up is used to lighten the skin on these women. The lighter their skin the more beautiful the Pakistani women appear to the men. Red lipstick, pink rouge, and dark "kohl" lining their eyes are applied heavily on each face. Kohl is a black substance used all over India and Pakistan to highlight both men and women's eyes. In some ways kohl is similar to eye liner that American women use every day. These women of ill repute wear low cut dresses with lots of silver and gold thread making them flash and sparkle in the low light. Women will beckon to the men and offer them delights beyond compare for only a few rupees. Ali took me into part of this neighborhood one evening and I was extremely shocked by my eye-opening experience there. Never having viewed a red-light district in my rather innocent life, this one certainly surprised me. I asked him how these women, being Muslim, would be allowed by the Mullahs to be prostitutes. He explained that in Islam there is a "hadith" or verse in the Qur'an which allows for temporary marriage or Mut'a. It seems that Muhammad knew that men wanted female companionship, especially when they were out conquering other countries, and he conveniently received a message from Allah one day about extremely short marriages. These marriages could be for weeks, days, or even minutes as the situation required for the man to have his sexual satisfaction. A man can pick out a particular woman and, after he has paid for her, he just has to say that they are married to her pimp. When he is finished with the woman, he must say three times that they are divorced. I was told that this "Mut'a" does not require documents or Mullahs or wedding ceremonies for it to be permitted in the eyes of the Muslim religious leaders and society. Of course, men are permitted to have multiple wives and concubines, so it is true that Muslim men can have their cake and eat it, too. In reality, this temporary marriage in Islam is just a way of allowing prostitution to exist. If the prostitute accidentally becomes pregnant, the man has no obligation to support the child. I suspect that these prostitutes are sophisticated in methods of birth control so that accidents rarely happen. If they do happen and a child is born the babies become members of the lowest rung of Pakistani society. Often the illegitimate boys will become beggars and the girls will be put into prostitution at a very early age, sometimes nine or ten years old. Before that age the girls will be used as servants and sweep floors for a living. The Prophet Muhammad had a nine year old wife, Aisha, when he was over 50 years old. Aisha was the daughter of one of his principal disciples. Apparently the 50 year old Prophet Muhammad did not hesitate to consummate his marriage to this nine year old girl immediately. Child marriage is not looked down on at all in orthodox Muslim countries. The practice of early marriage continues to this day in many Muslim countries even though the girls can suffer severe injuries from early intercourse and childbirth. Rape is a different matter altogether in the Muslim world. Actually it is difficult to prove rape in any Muslim country. The Prophet Muhammad said that in order for a woman to prove that she was raped by a man there has to be four adult male Muslim, not Christian, witnesses to the actual sexual penetration. Many readers can understand why no woman can prove she has been raped in Islamic countries, even if she becomes pregnant from this rape.

I could tell that Ali was nervous and on guard when we started to venture into this particular neighborhood. I was not wearing a burkah or dark veil and men began looking at me the further we ventured into the alleys. Soon he felt it was unsafe for me to be on these streets unveiled, so we turned off to another, safer area of the district. I had seen enough in the few minutes of our journey to understand much concerning the status of these women in Pakistan. Women were used for sex by many types of men. There were both rich and poor men wandering the streets looking carefully at the women who displayed themselves in doors or windows. All of these women had Pakistani pimps who would do the bartering with the men after they make their choice. A "char pi" or small bed was set up in the tiny room on the other side of the door that the woman stood at to attract her customer. When she is occupied with a client, she closes a curtain in front of the door for those few minutes. A passerby can usually hear what is happening behind the curtain as you walk through these streets. The earthy noises are sometimes drowned out by loud music from the radios or tape players that are being piped into the area by small shop owners who run the refreshment stands nearby. Not all of the individuals behind the doors are women. Some of the prostitutes were small, delicate young boys who were made-up to resemble girls, with long hair, saris, or very sheer dresses barely covering their child-like boyish bodies. You could buy anything for a moment's pleasure in this "red light" district. This was years before the age of AIDS, although I expect many other diseases were rampant here. Women, young girls, and boys were treated as objects for men's pleasure and sold every minute for small amounts of money.

Also inside this same gate of the walled city is one of the world's largest mosques, the Badshahi Masjid. At a later time Ali and his mother took me to see the beauty of the walls and ceiling inside this mosque. I was told to take off my shoes and cover my head when I entered the holy door. Minarets are located on each of the corners of the four walls and the Mullahs sing their hypnotic calls to prayer from the tops of these graceful structures. The walls are inlaid with Ivory and precious stones in Islamic script adorning the columns and public areas. All the fabulous mosques were built by the famous Moghul emperors in the 16th and 17th centuries. The architecture is magnificent and cannot possibly be equaled by any modern Islamic structures.

That day we were in the old city only to shop for cloth and we must go to the Anarkali Bazaar, a neighborhood reserved for the shop keepers. Anarkali bazaar is the most interesting of the city's many bazaars. The alleys and lanes of this market place are where many exciting shops, especially traditional crafts like leather wear, embroidered garments, bangles, gold and silver jewelry, creations in silk, and the cloth merchants are located.

We ventured through hundreds of small shops in rows filled with different items for sale. These shops were made of wood and built wall-to-wall in a long line. One entire block was made up of small stores filled with embroidered shawls, one entire block was gold jewelry and gemstones, one block held stores with only silver jewelry, and one block was stalls filled with shoes of every kind. Finally we came to the shops brimming with bolts of cloth.

We chose one of the small stores whose shopkeeper had been recommended to us by Ali's brother and entered it by the small door. The shop keeper immediately offered us a place to sit and sent his ten year old assistant for some chai tea. He closed a curtain which hung in front of the door to the shop for privacy. This signified to the general public that this shop was occupied with a female customer. Chai tea is tea boiled with milk and sugar and is usually overly sweet. Rolls and rolls of fantastic silk and satin were unfurled in front of me and draped over my lap and legs. I was completely surrounded with colors and soft fabric. I felt as if I was in heaven and wanted to purchase all of the cloth and take it home with me. Some of it was plain with no embroidery; some of it was ornate and filled with different colored threads. We went through approximately sixty bolts of cloth, one at a time, and held it up to my face to see if it suited my light coloring. I finally chose a light blue silk with only a small amount of gold trim woven into the fabric. It was not too flashy and could be used for a variety of social functions after the tea party. The shop keeper cut off about six yards and wrapped it up. He thanked us in Urdu many times for our purchase, bowing at the waist, and told us to return soon.

We then left his shop and walked again down the rows of small stores until we found one where shoes were sold. The earlier shopping procedure was repeated and I soon selected a pair of slippers that was trimmed in gold thread and had gold tips. After that we went back out of the bazaar with our cloth wrapped in plain newspaper with a string tying it shut. The shoes were wrapped in another piece of newspaper. I thought it was a terrific recycling of old newsprint and just as good as fancy shopping bags.

We caught a taxi which drove us to a tailor's shop near our apartment outside the old city. This tailor's shop was small with three sewing machines on the floor and the tailors seated on the floor in front of each machine. Piles of partially sewn wool and silk suits and dresses surrounded the tailors as they worked. Ali did all the talking and introduced us both to one of the tailors. He explained that we needed a rather modern design of chemise and pajama (pants) and they must be finished in a week. Immediately the tailor went into the back room and brought out a book with photos and cut-out magazine pictures for us to look over for a specific design. I looked carefully through the pages and finally chose a modern design with straight legs instead of baggie pants and a rather tight fitting dress. Movie stars in India and Pakistan dressed in the tighter clothes and this particular outfit was the perfect design for a slim twenty year old girl. Ali approved my choice of designs, also feeling it was appropriate for a tea party with other Americans involved. Then, as my husband watched, the male tailor was allowed to measure me in various places on my body. He carefully, without touching me, measured my leg length, my instep, my waist, my hips, my bust, and my shoulders. After each measurement he wrote it down on a piece of paper in Urdu. He never said a single word to me and never once looked into my eyes or face. It was almost as if I was a plastic mannequin instead of a real human being. He took the blue silk cloth from us and told Ali in Urdu it would be ready in several days. When our order was delivered to our home, I was impressed; the entire chemise and pants were exactly like the magazine photo I had shown the tailor, and they fit perfectly. This outfit cost about $15.00, including the tailor's bill of about $7.00. After I found a matching long scarf for my head, I was ready for the tea party at the ambassador's house.

The tea party was held at about 2:00 o'clock on a Sunday afternoon. Ali brought me in a taxi to a neighborhood that was surrounded by a large iron fence and gate. There were guards at the gate and I had to show the invitation before the taxi was able to enter. I was amazed by my surroundings when we drove through the gate. The entire area was filled with mansions, beautiful flowers, and wide manicured lawns. This was the American compound and my first experience with a gated community. The mansions surrounding the Ambassadors home were all magnificent. They were provided by the American government to many who worked at the American Consulate in Lahore. These families lived in complete luxury with servants, cooks, drivers, and gardeners, probably far superior living conditions compared to how they had lived somewhere in Washington DC. It was surprising to view the neighborhood, a place of tranquility far away from the real Pakistan, but nestled in the heart of Lahore. The taxi let me out at the front door of the Ambassador's home. The large white building was situated down a circular driveway which curled under an entrance area used in case of rain or to shield from the hot sun.

A servant opened the door of the taxi on my side while Ali stayed with the taxi driver. I got out and walked toward the large, imposing front door.   A strange feeling of separation of the worlds of east and west occurred as I walked away from the two men and into the mansion. I felt like I was walking into another world. At the door stood a turbaned Punjabi, over six feet tall, wearing a perfectly white Nehru jacket and white pants, with pointed turned up gold shoes. He resembled someone from the movie "Rains of Ranchipur" a 1955 Hollywood movie starring Lana Turner and Richard Burton, set in India. I had seen this movie several times on the late, late show on television. It was very impressive to see this man standing by the door, and as I approached, he leaned over and opened it for me to enter. As I moved inside, a middle aged woman descended upon me with a smile on her face and introduced herself as the Ambassador's wife.   There were many middle aged American women in the room, dressed exactly as my mother might dress or resembling June Cleaver from the television show "Leave it to Beaver", with flowered dresses, hose and high healed, light colored shoes. I was the only woman in the room dressed as a modern Pakistani girl. The room was quite large with windows all around and iron bars painted white stretching across each window. It looked as if I had just walked into a room at the White House in

Washington D.C. The Ambassador's wife made a comment to me that more of the American women should dress in traditional Pakistani garb because it was so beautiful. I said some type of mumbled polite statement to her in agreement, for I knew immediately that she was just trying to put me at my ease. This was the only sentence that she ever uttered to me during the entire tea party. The tea service was set up in the next room where the grand piano was located. Other American women were pouring tea and passing out cookies and cakes. The Muslim servants were also serving cups of tea with white cloth napkins. The seal of the United States of America was embroidered delicately on each napkin. The servants were men, and all wore white gloves just as black house servants used to do in some Southern parts of the United States. Several women were polite to me, but I believe that they were not happy that I was married to a Pakistani man. Their husbands all worked for the Embassy and this was their little closed, snobbish society. Many Americans were new to Pakistan because of the beginning of the Nixon administration in America in January 1969. For a single moment in time I was reminding them that this was another country. A very different society was located only yards away, outside their gated American community. I had broken some unwritten law by wearing clothing that was native to this country instead of my American clothes.

I was extremely polite; my mother and grandmother had taught me carefully while growing up how to behave at parties, and I made small talk with those women around me who would engage in conversation. Some of the servants glanced at me and I was sure that the Punjabi footmen and other servants were wondering why an American girl would dress this way in the home of the American Ambassador. The servants never spoke a word during the entire party, never ask questions or made any comments to anyone, and never looked into any woman's face. They served silently and left the room immediately when they finished their job. I gave my Lahore address to a few of the younger American women, but never heard from any of them later. Someone mentioned to me of a job opening at the American School if I was interested in working part time.

There had been political processions by college students and labor strikes several weeks earlier in Lahore. College students were supporting some particular political party or ideal. The procession had gotten out of hand and violence resulted near the American Embassy. A car had been turned over and set fire to by the wild mob. The women at the tea party referred to this "riot" and asked if I was afraid living in the area of town near the university. The American women were nervous and afraid because of the incident, and some were thinking of leaving and going back to the states. I told them I was not afraid because I was surrounded by Pakistanis every day and night. I knew several professors, had visited the university, talked to students, and met poor people and rich people during the few months I lived in Pakistan. None of these violent incidents frightened me. At that time I was not worried about any of the political changes affecting my living conditions or making me wish to return to America. Weren't students in America doing exactly the same thing, but for different reasons? Weren't youth around the world trying to change their own countries to make life for their citizens more equitable? I told them that I was not afraid, and they stared back at me as if I, too, were a foreigner with strange ideas. I quickly realized that I was in the midst of a group of women who did not understand anything about this country. They all lived in semi-seclusion with their American friends and only saw the local Pakistani people as servants or tradesmen. I lived in Lahore as a Pakistani bride and was quickly learning the language and customs. I saw a different population of people whom they would never meet. In about one hour I excused myself and quietly left the Ambassador's home.

Ali had waited for me outside in the taxi the entire time I had been at the tea party. I was very relieved to be away from the Ambassadors house and these women who had never mentally left Washington, D.C. As I walked through the door of the house I did notice the Punjabi footmen slightly glancing at me, and I believe he was fascinated at my dress and assimilation into Lahore culture. I am sure he did not see Americans dress this way often and was probably surprised by this young American woman observing local traditions. I offered him a traditional greeting in Urdu "Salaam Al Akim" and he answered back the appropriate response, "Wow Akim Salaam". I then walked from the house to the taxi and returned to the real life I was living in Pakistan.

I began to understand what the "Ugly American" designation was all about during this tea party. American families lived and worked here in Lahore, never getting to know their servants, never understanding why or how this Muslim society worked the way I was observing it. The servants were paid small amounts of money for their work in the American homes and embassy. Generally, American embassy workers had no friends who were Pakistani or even visited Pakistani homes. Americans did not invite Pakistanis to their homes or serve them tea and cakes in the afternoon. They lived in fear of the native population in Lahore and kept them out of their lives entirely. The only information Americans received was from their own government, filtered with whatever political propaganda was the mode of the day.

Later that year the Americans sent Neil Armstrong to the moon. He turned out to be the first human to ever walk on the moon. The date for the historic moon walk was July 20, 1969. It was in all the newspapers in Lahore on the front page in large letters. No one that I talked to in Pakistan ever believed that it really happened. Shahji came to our house that day and talked to me about the moon walk. He slammed the newspaper on the kitchen table and laughed heartily! He told me he believed that it was a Hollywood stunt, done by America to fool the world. He said it could not be done and believed it was probably a sin according to the Qur'an. He then proceeded to recite an Arabic verse or two that meant anyone who attempted to go to the moon would be killed or destroyed instantly by Allah. I tried to explain to him that it had been done by America, that we were scientifically advanced, and asked him why he thought we would want to fool the world into thinking we had accomplished this task. I also commented that somehow Allah has held back his punishment for the errant space travelers and allowed them to return to America in safety. Shahji asked that if America was so scientifically advanced and rich why they didn't help the poor of the world instead of sending a space ship to the moon. This was a good question and I wasn't prepared to answer it. All I was able to respond was that I did not know why America spent money this way except to accomplish scientific exploration. I'm sure that Pakistan was not the only country at the time who believed Americans never walked on the moon.

If you want to understand why Muslim people around the world currently hate America you must begin to understand the Islamic life style and history. Islam totally controls their lives and customs. Americans do not need to believe what Pakistani's believe, or treat their wives and sisters as women are treated in these countries, just understand how Muslims think and learn more about their history. Americans often believe we are superior to the people in the "third" world who are usually dark skinned, poor, and under educated.

Lahore is a very interesting city to visit or live in, with many historic architectural wonders. When I arrived in Pakistan the President of the country was a military man named Ayub Khan who had kept Pakistan under martial law for many months. He had several attempts made on his life by assassins, and withdrew behind a curtain of dictatorship, becoming a remote figure in a bullet proof limousine. In February 1969 Ayub Khan announced he would not stop elections which were scheduled for 1970. Protests by students were everywhere in Lahore because people wanted elections immediately. I was not allowed to be near any of them, but saw one from the roof top of our home one afternoon with Babur. The procession was filled with young men holding banners and placards and chanting something I did not understand. They walked six abreast and the procession was about one mile long. The military police watched them carefully, but did not disturb them. There was no violence during this particular demonstration. Babur told me that it consisted mostly of students who wished for a new, non-military government to be formed.

In March 1969 Ayub Khan resigned and handed the Presidency over to another army general – Agha Mohammed Yahya Khan. Again the country was placed under martial law. This martial law only affected me in small and uneventful ways. There were curfews at night and sometimes we needed to avoid large crowds of people. Occasionally the university was closed for short periods of time. These closures stopped classes and gave Ali more time to show me some of the interesting sites in Lahore.

The old walled city was at the center of Lahore and had grown over many centuries. Because space is limited within the great wall, the houses and shops are all close together. Cobblestone walk ways or alleys are throughout the walled city, and the human sewage runs in a narrow open trough down the center of these walk ways. I often saw children squat over an open sewer to urinate or defecate into the street. Men opened their tie belt, turned toward the walls, and proceeded to urinate in public any time they felt the urge. No one blinks an eye or thinks anything of this action that would land them in jail in most cities in America. I even saw women, entirely clothed in a black burkah, squatting over a sewer urinating. You could only see their black tent shaped material with a mesh strip where the eyes are located, but nothing else showed on their bodies. Of course, as we passed nearby we could certainly hear what was going on under their burkahs. The streets were filthy and narrow in the walled city. There are four large gates to the city: Roshnai Gate, Masti Gate, Bhati Gate, and Delhi Gate, which in years past kept invaders out of the old city. Now these large gates remain open and are impressive to a foreigner.

The houses in this area are old and dark. Many buildings were over 200 years old in this part of town. Ali's childhood home was here and his brother still lived in the three story house with his eleven children. Houses were constructed out of concrete blocks, brick, or an adobe mud-like material baked hard in the sun to dry. We visited this neighborhood many times during my stay in Lahore. Each time I visited I was amazed at the culture and filth of the neighborhood. I would be asked to go with family members to have tea with a relative or friend and never refused this invitation. It was fascinating for me to see these other homes and life styles. The old walled city was a much more conservative part of Lahore.

Lahore established itself as the capital of the Punjab in the year 1001 AD and began to play a major role as a seat of Muslim power and influence in those years. The city grew behind the walls as the population expanded. Outside the walls of the city is Lahore Fort. In the early 16th century, Lahore was greatly influenced by the Moghul rulers. The Moghul Emperor Akbar re-built Lahore Fort from mud walls to solid brick in 1566 and enlarged the fort toward the north of the walled city. The fort surrounds approximately thirty acres of land, gardens and marble structures. The buildings and beautiful work by artisans are outstanding examples of Moghul art at its height. It was awe inspiring to see the inlaid marble and intricately carved lattice work intended for both protection and areas where women of the harem could look out unseen by men. There are fountains, marble tables, and mosaic tiled rooms in most of the Fort.

One of the most impressive places is the Shish Mahal or Palace of Mirrors. It is located on the north side of the fort and has a row of high domed rooms. Every ceiling in the rooms is covered with hundreds of thousands of tiny mirrors inlaid into the marble. This mirror decoration and design is referred to as "Shishgari". If you light a cigarette lighter inside the Palace of Mirrors it immediately throws back a million reflections. I enjoyed fantasizing about what Shah Jehan was doing in these rooms with his harem. Ali and I walked through the Lahore Fort one spring afternoon and I was enthralled with the magnificence that still exists today even though it was built approximately four hundred years ago. It was as if I had stepped back in time into the Arabian nights or court of a Sultan.

The Emperor Shah Jehan lived in Lahore for periods of time with his favorite wife Mumtaz Mahal before she died in 1631. She died giving birth to their fourteenth child, and he was heartbroken to lose her. After her death he decided to build the Taj Mahal as her tomb. The Taj Mahal is located in the city of Agra, India. The tomb was not completed until 1643 and is considered one of the wonders of the world and a master piece of Moghul architecture and art. It is said to show the great love that this one man had for his favorite wife, for Shah Jahan had many wives and concubines. Lahore is located at a much higher elevation than the scorching hot plains of India and would often serve as the summer residence for Moghul Emperors to help escape the heat. Because of this there are many beautiful structures built by the Moghuls in and around Lahore. Lahore is regarded in Pakistan as the cultural, architectural, and artistic center of the country.

It was extremely difficult for me to understand why any American citizen, given the chance to see and learn about this interesting city, would not dive in and soak it up as I was doing. I suppose no American would feel safe visiting the old walled city unescorted by someone born in that area. But I visited it many times and never had any encounters with danger or violence. The opportunity is everywhere, in Lahore, to find out fascinating information about a culture totally different than the American lifestyle.

CHAPTER 6: THE ROAD FROM KARACHI

Nine months earlier when Ali had purchased the Volkswagen Beetle automobile in Germany, he had no idea that it would take so long for the freighter to reach Karachi. The car had to be shipped from Germany to Karachi, Pakistan, and when it got there a letter was sent out of the Karachi Port Authority notifying him that it had arrived and a large duty or import tax placed on it. The automobile had arrived on a ship and was being held in customs until he paid about fifteen hundred dollars to have it released to him. There was no other choice than to make the trip to Karachi, pay the duty to get the car out of the customs holding area, and drive it back to Lahore. It was March 1969, and Ali decided to travel by train to Karachi to pick up the car. This was not as simple as it might seem to any westerner. The drive back from Karachi was through some pretty wild open spaces and rough small towns. This trip was over one thousand miles of bad road and the possibility of bandits or "dacoits" lying in wait along the way. Ali did not want to be caught alone on the road with a blonde American woman by bandits known to be in the area. Dacoits carry guns and are known to kidnap foreigners and especially young women from the regional villages to hold them for ransom. Once again he asked two of his adult cousins to travel with us to Karachi and accompany us on the trip back to Lahore for protection. At Punjab University it was spring break and the perfect time for the trip. We had a week to get to Karachi, release the car from customs, see a little of the country, and return to Lahore. It was going to be a full and interesting week.

Trains in Pakistan all looked as if they were built before the 1930's. This train's cars had curved wooden and metal roofs, wooden trim at the doors and windows, and flat wooden benches inside to sit on. It reminded me of trains in old western movies which used to be on TV in America. Some areas inside the train had no seats and were filled with extremely poor women and children sitting on the dirty metal floor. The mothers sat with their young children on their saris or pajamas and fed them "roti" or flat bread made out of wheat. Many of the young children had shaved heads and sad faces. They looked at me with awe when I walked through the train car. Their shaved heads indicated that they had been sick recently and the parents had taken them to the barber to get rid of their hair. If a child was sick and had long hair, the parents believed that it would sap the strength from their children; so many parents immediately shave their sick children's heads to help them get well faster. It was also believed that their hair would grow back much stronger after it was shaved than before they were ill. There was a high mortality rate among young children in Pakistan at this time. Approximately one third of Pakistani children were born without basic healthcare, inoculations, cleanliness, or the help of physicians, and would die before they were two years old.

We were in the second class compartment of the train, with wooden benches for seats. There were no comfortable padded seats in any area of the train that I was able to observe from where I was seated. Maybe there was something better in the First Class area, but once again we could not afford this type of luxury for a train ride. We had packed a single small suitcase for the two of us to share. Ali carried it on the train. It held several changes of clothes, plus any personal care products we might need. It sat on the floor under our feet and we both guarded it carefully while on the train because theft was a possibility. .

The trip would take approximately fifteen hours, so we would be riding, sitting up, on wooden benches for the overnight ride. We boarded the train at approximately 1:30 in the afternoon on a Saturday. After waiting on our bench inside the compartment for one hour the train began to move slowly out of the station. I was told by Ali that trains were rarely on time in Pakistan since the British left India. There were many tiresome stops along the way at various towns where additional people would board the train and some would get off. I could watch from the window while entire families of men, women, and children would disembark from the train holding bundles of clothes and belongings. The bundles were not luggage like a European or Westerner might use to carry clothing, but large cotton sheets wrapped around everything, tied in a knot and slung over the man or woman's back. It looked heavy and uncomfortable, but many poor people carried their extra clothing this way when traveling. They did not have the money for purchasing suitcases or back packs. Ali's two cousins, Mahmood and Akbar, who were big, strapping, handsome Punjabi men, rode in another car where many young men sat without being near women. We had packed food in a metal container, similar to a lunch box, for refreshments during the trip. We also had a thermos with tea for drinking along the way. A passenger could buy food and drink from vendors on the train, but we could not be sure of the quality and I did not want to get ill by eating or drinking anything sold to us by tradespeople. We were seated on one of the wooden benches near a window, no cushions or pillows available to pad the wood. I had brought a small cotton blanket and when it was doubled up we had something to pad the bench. It was hard and uncomfortable, but we endured it for the next 15 hours. The only bathroom was in the corner of the railway car and had a wooden door on it. Both men and women used the same toilet and it stank so much it was hard to get used to visiting it. The waste from the bathroom flowed out on the railroad track and was spread over the entire thousand mile trip. No toilet paper or water for washing was available on the train. After a long night of the train noise, smelly bodies, and little sleep, we arrived in Karachi early the next morning and immediately took a taxi to the house of Ali's friend. The two male cousins went their own way for a day or two of partying in Karachi. The young men were going to stay in local guest hostels. We would meet them after we had picked up the automobile so they could accompany us on the ride back to Lahore. I heard stories from Ali of their excitement to be in

Karachi with plenty of movie houses and exotic entertainment for men to enjoy. They would also purchase a small pistol on the black market of Karachi. It was a .38 caliber pistol that they found from a gun merchant in one of the dark alley ways of the city. Ali had given them the money to buy the weapon and bullets before the trip, and they knew exactly where to find the right one. Most Pathan tribesmen from the border region with Afghanistan knew how to shoot guns, but these cousins were "city boys" from Lahore, and I was not sure if they had ever even had any target practice with a pistol. I did not even know if Ali would understand how to handle a gun if any bandits attacked our car, but I felt a little safer knowing the two cousins were armed. I was not worried about them being bored during our small separation for the next two days. These men were adults and would find night clubs and dancing girls to entertain them. This situation was a little bit like two country boys coming from Kansas to visit New York City for a few days. They would find plenty of activity to keep them busy. I believe anything they did in Karachi for this short trip would not be reported to their father, so they were pretty free to be wild and have a good time.

Our accommodations were at the home of one of Ali's friends whom he had met at the university, and it turned out to be one of the most comfortable places we had visited so far in Pakistan. The family we were going to stay with was named Zubari, and the house was surrounded by a high concrete wall. It was a nice residence with about 2,000 square feet of living space in the home. A beautiful walled garden was in back with blooming flowers and various small gardens surrounding a covered porch. There were four bedrooms, a living room and dining room plus a spacious kitchen. The kitchen had an extra large store room for rice, flour, lentils, and other dry grain metal storage containers. A western gas stove, not a double burner camping stove like in our kitchen, was situated on one wall and the kitchen had wooden counters on either side. Several servants were employed to do the cooking and cleaning for the family. It was certainly a modern household compared to the one we lived at in Lahore. The family consisted of the husband, Dr. Ahmed Zubari, his wife, and two unmarried daughters. The large roomy house had marble floors, high white walls, and ceiling fans always whirling to keep a breeze in the home. Karachi was a much warmer climate than Lahore because it was lower in altitude and on the Indus plain. The average temperature during the day in March was around 85 degrees. Karachi is on the coast of the Arabian Sea and, while there is a breeze, the weather is often humid.

We were met at the door by the family and after some greetings and excitement; we were shown to our guest bedroom. The room assigned to us was located down a long narrow hallway and was quite large. The bed had a real queen sized spring mattress on a bed frame, not a char-pi. There were large pillows and a cotton bedspread for the bed. The bed sheets matched and were of a soft Egyptian cotton so my face would not be rubbed raw. In the corner of the room was a door leading to a comfortable large bathroom with shower and toilet. This bathroom appeared especially luxurious to me. Red Afghan pile rugs were on the light colored marble floor of the bedroom and there were two wooden tables beside the bed, both with reading lamps placed on them. On one of the bedroom walls hung an oil painting of a city scene in Karachi. The painting was roughly done, but with bright colors, and it depicted an interesting group of buildings with a single man sweeping the street in front of a building with a broom. A vase with large yellow flowers was placed on a narrow table along one wall. The entire room before me was comfortable and inviting. I felt as if I had just received an unexpected gift from this family by staying a few nights in their bedroom.

It was time for lunch when we arrived so we unpacked quickly, showered, changed our clothes, and joined the family in the dining room. Lunch consisted of rice with lentils, curried chicken, and flat bread. Chicken was considered an expensive dish to serve to guests, so this food was indeed a compliment. It was brought from the kitchen in a beautiful English serving bowl with a lid and put on the table by one of the young male servants. We were given lukewarm tea to drink; ice was not used in tea even though it was very warm weather in Karachi at this time. The entire family was college educated and knew fluent English, so the conversation was lively and fun. The girls were not in any way inhibited by Ali being in the room. They were both attending the local college. These two unmarried daughters were within a few years of my age and became quite friendly with me. Visiting with this family made me begin to believe that people were similar all over the world.

They addressed Ali as "Uncle" because of his friendship with their father. Their father was a college professor who made a pretty good income from his job. It was certainly enough money to comfortably support his wife and send his daughters to college. The girls did not dress in burkahs or the black veils so prevalent in Lahore even though they were Muslim, and wore either saris or a modern style chemise and pants outfits. They were good examples of modern Pakistani women growing up in a less restricted society than Lahore's young women appeared to be living in. It seemed to me as if Karachi was a much more modern and sophisticated city and not as conservative as people seemed to be in Lahore. While I might hesitate to refer to Karachi as cosmopolitan during this time, I would say that women did have more freedom and opportunities for work and education then in the city of Lahore.

The next day was Monday and Ali left me early in the morning to visit the ship yards and inquire about the automobile and how to get it released from customs. It took him all day to go through the paperwork and pay off the car duty. I'm sure he had to grease a few palms, or pay baksheesh, in order to have things go smoothly. He never told me how much it cost to get the car out of Karachi customs, but it was plenty of rupees. By dinner time he was able to drive back to the house with his new Volkswagen. He had filled up the car with gasoline at one of the many "petrol" stations around Karachi. There was a parking area within the high concrete wall of the house, so the car would be safe all night.

During the day when Ali was trying to get possession of the car, I proceeded to learn more about the young Zubari girls. Their names were Shashi and Liala; we talked about America for hours and what women did in school and work. They were curious about women's freedoms and how people in America decided to marry for love. I explained American dating customs to them and they filled me in on some of Pakistan's traditions concerning women. They were good Muslim girls and did not believe in wearing revealing clothes or sleeping with men before marriage. They expected their father and mother to arrange their marriages for them when they were ready and proper young men were found. They also enjoyed motion pictures and tried to go to movies whenever they were not in school or studying for tests. They read English literature and enjoyed books of all kinds. Both girls hoped to find love in their future marriages, but would never consider dating without their parents consent. They expected to meet their prospective husbands before marriage in chaperoned settings with their parents. Each girl went to a women's college in Karachi and made high marks. One daughter was thinking of becoming a teacher, while the other was trying to complete a business degree. This education would enable her to work in an office somewhere in Karachi.

I was tired and finally took some time to have a nap during the afternoon. I had not gotten much sleep on the train the night before. On the drive back to Lahore I might not get much sleep, either, because we would be trying to make the fastest time possible on our return trip.

Ali arrived back at the house in the late afternoon with his new gray Volkswagen Beetle. We all had to go outside to look it over and admire it. We were preparing to leave the next morning for our long road trip, so after Ali arrived with the car we decided to pick up a few food items that would not easily spoil in the heat.

There were some wonderful open air markets with a large variety of fruits not too far from the Zubari house. Both Zubari girls decided to drive with us, in the back seat, to the market, and we were able to walk around freely to pick out some oranges, pears, and varieties of fruit I did not recognize, for the journey. We also found a tin of English biscuits while searching some of the shops in the bazaar. These would be good snacks for part of the trip, so we purchased our supplies and returned to the Zubari home for dinner. Dinner had been prepared by the servants when we arrived and all of the family happily sat down to curried lamb and spinach, rice, lentil cakes, and "roti" or flat wheat bread. There was always plain yogurt at every meal and I began to acquire a taste for putting it on rice or curry to dull the spices. The dinner was delicious and not too spicy for my tastes. Servants cleared the table afterwards and we retired to the living room to talk about the trip home. Dr. Zubari suggested we try to visit Moenjodaro on our way back to Lahore. He told us stories of interesting archeological ruins discovered and excavated in 1922 approximately 300 miles from Karachi. This area sounded like an educational and fascinating side trip for our group to visit.

Early the next morning, after our farewells to the Zubari family, we drove to the youth hostel to pick up Mahmood and Akbar and started on our journey. The .38 caliber pistol was secretly slid under the car seat but close enough for Mahmood to grab if needed. Mahmood and Akbar were about six foot two or taller, 180 lbs, with broad shoulders. Punjabi men are known for their fighting abilities and bravery during battles. Both of the cousins were in their mid twenties and seemed capable of hurting any bandit who might decide to rob us or kidnap me. I felt comfortable having them along for the ride even though they did not speak much English and we had few conversations during our trip.

It was decided that we would try to visit Moenjodaro. The highways out of Karachi were not in good condition and only two lanes wide. While our car could go much faster than 60 miles per hour, it was not easy to do so on this road. There were plenty of pot-holes and also much foot traffic with ox-carts filled with hay and other horse drawn wagons, all clogging up the roadway. There was no such thing on these highways as sheriff's cars or policemen trying to stop you for driving too fast or for any reason at all. Motorists took their chances when driving from city to city in Pakistan. All of these road problems slowed automobile traffic down to a medium or slow speed. It would take us slightly less than six hours to get to Moenjodaro, which would put us there at about 3:00 in the afternoon. There were plenty of gas stations along the main road from Karachi to Lahore because it was a major truck route for carrying supplies in land to Lahore and from there to other cities.

Our plan was to visit the archeological site for an hour or two and then move on to a nearby town to spend the night. Moenjodaro is located on the right bank of the Indus River in Pakistan's Sindh Province. It flourished for about eight hundred years during the third and second millennium B.C. As center of the Indus civilization and one of the largest cities in the old world, this five thousand year old city is the earliest manifestation of urbanization in south Asia. It now consists of quite a large amount of flat land acreage which is now excavated ruins that surpass many other oriental civilizations' archeological sites. The structural remains of Moenjodaro was discovered and excavated in 1922. It was threatened with decay by exposure to harsh floods from the Indus River for many years after its important excavation. At the time I visited these ruins, forty years after their discovery, a team of archaeologists has been working on saving what they could from the area but were having problems with funding their work. Many years later I learned that this site had been declared a World Heritage site and was saved by an increase in worldwide funding for rebuilding because of this prestigious designation. Located near Moenjodaro was a small museum filled with pottery, necklaces and utensils found at the site. The jewelry was especially fascinating because it was made of simply worked pure gold bracelets, necklaces, and rings. Some of the jewelry had rough cut emeralds imbedded in the gold. I toured the area with great interest and viewed as much as I could in the short few hours that I was allowed to be a tourist.

After visiting Moenjodaro we drove about an hour to the nearby town of Rohri. We found food and chai tea in a small road side market. It was a little village and had a single motel or guest house with dirty rooms and flea infested sheets spread out on the char pies available to us. We purchased one room with four char pis in it and all bunked together for safety that night. The windows had bars, but no glass, on them, but it did not look like a secure establishment so we decided to all sleep in the same room. The room had a rather small bathroom with a sink and toilet. We were able to park the Volkswagen right outside our bedroom window so that the men could keep an eye on it. We brought our luggage and gun, wrapped in a cloth, into the room for safety and did not leave anything in the car over night. Because the sheets and beds were so dirty we took the mattresses off of them and piled them in a corner of the room. Everyone slept in their travel clothes for the entire evening. Each of us curled up on our own bare char pi ropes and stuffed our suitcases or bundles under our heads for pillows. I had the same small cotton blanket that I had used as padding on the train ride to Karachi. It covered me, but the weather was warm that evening and none of us really needed blankets. The night was without incident, although sleeping was not so easy on the uncomfortable beds. We had rented the room for security, as our only other option was to sleep sitting up in the car all night. Early the next morning we ate some boiled eggs, rice, and tea that we purchased from a road side cafe and immediately started out again on the road. We wanted to cover many miles this day and headed for Bahawalpur, about 175 miles away from Rohri. As we drove down the road I watched the countryside with interest. This land was made up of rich farm lands, water buffalos, and flat roofed houses with mud brick walls around them for protection from bandits. I enjoyed watching the children and the country people doing their daily work around their homes. This was a primitive area; it was near to the Sutlej River and seemed to be very fertile for growing crops. Dates and mangoes are also grown in this region of Pakistan. Canals are used for irrigation, and the children are always swimming in the water or women could be seen washing clothes on the banks. In the country side women did not wear the burkah as much as in cities. They would still not walk too near men and often covered their faces with brightly colored cotton cloth or shawls. I watched for horses but rarely saw anything more than a skinny pony standing in a field or pulling a cart. I had seen a few beautiful horses in Lahore at the polo grounds, but out here in the country the animals looked as if they were mistreated and malnourished. The main work animal was the water buffalo, and it was used for pulling carts and plowing fields. We saw lots of children pulling the family water buffalo into a canal and washing them off in the late afternoon. The buffalos seemed to enjoy the bath and would calmly allow children to ride on their back and play around their flanks while being washed.

Often we were passed by large trucks called Lorries, being driven much faster than our small car. Buses filled with people were on the narrow roads, also. These buses had men and luggage on the roof as well as inside on the seats. The women usually rode inside the buses if they could find a seat. Sometimes you would see a young man hanging off the side with only his left hand and arm gripping the side of the bus. I believe they were illegally riding the bus and had not paid a fare. Buses and trucks swayed precariously as they sped past our little car. They were painted with bright colors and pictures along each side of the bus, often advertising a movie that was being shown in theatres. The Lorries were usually speeding and driven recklessly around us on the road. Ali had to drive carefully so that we would not be involved in a wreck with these vehicles. Driving was done on the left side of the road like the British custom. This made it difficult for me to take over and relieve Ali during the trip. I had never driven on the left side of the road and it made me nervous. I was also afraid to drive the car because the trucks and buses were speeding and seemed especially dangerous to small cars like ours. The two men with us, Mahmood and Akbar, did not know how to drive. Neither man owned a car back in Lahore, nor was driving something they had learned from anyone of their acquaintance. So the burden of the driving fell on Ali, and he had not gotten much sleep the night before. We stopped a few times at small villages for hot chai to refresh us. Coffee was only available in large cities in Pakistan so we could not easily get a good stimulating cup of it. Any time one of us had to urinate we just stopped along the side of the road and went behind a bush. I was always nervous about cobras or other snakes which were known to be in India and Pakistan. I took the blanket with me and Ali would hold it around me and turn his head while I urinated in semi-private conditions along the road side. There was nothing else to do but keep moving as fast as we could from small town to small town. We were hoping that any bandits in the countryside did not hear of us until we were long gone from the area.

At Multan we pulled over to get something to eat. Multan is an extremely old city which has seen a lot of warfare in its history. The earliest history of Multan dates back to the time of Alexander the Great, around 334 B.C. At approximately 1300 A.D., Multan had served as the regional capital under a Sultan. The area around the city is a flat plain and is ideal for agriculture. There are many canals that cut across the Multan district that provide water from nearby rivers. At road side cafes we could always find rice cooking and other food available to purchase. I was able to get some cooked vegetables like peas to mix with my rice for an interesting lunch. Of course, the men and Ali had no difficulty finding hot curry or other spicy food that they loved. I had tried to eat spicy food in the past and now knew to steer clear of the hot spice filled mixtures because this food would make me ill.

Multon is located near the Chenab River and is a leading manufacturing town for silks, cotton, carpets and glazed pottery. We did not have extra money with us, so we were not interested in shopping, although many of the rugs hanging from walls of shops looked exceptionally beautiful to me. We decided to keep going as far as we could and try to reach Lahore that evening.

We headed toward Faisalabad, approximately one hundred fifty miles away from Multon. The Punjab is known as the land of the five rivers and we had already crossed the Indus River, the Chenab River, and the Ravi River. The five rivers flow out of the Himalayan Mountains and make the Punjab one of the most fertile areas on the India continent. Faisalabad is a city along the Chenab River which is considered an industrial center because of the railroad and industrial plants that mill cotton, sugar, flour, and canned fruit. We arrived there about 3:00 o'clock in the afternoon and took a much needed break for tea and small cakes at a small rest stop by the side of the road. Big cities such as Faisalabad had gas stations available for trucks and cars so we filled the tank up with gasoline and decided to head toward Lahore, which should only be about 150 miles down the road. All of us were tired and worn out, but decided to continue so we could sleep in our own beds that night. We climbed back into the Volkswagen and drove rapidly toward Lahore.

We finally entered the streets of Lahore at around 6:30 or 7:00 o'clock at night. It was dark already as we left Mahmood and Akbar off at the Bhati Gate in the old walled city of Lahore. Both men were happy to be safely home and ran off toward their houses with smiles on their faces. They took the gun tightly wrapped in a cloth with them as they left our vehicle. They both lived in houses which were located near Ali's brother's house in the old walled city. We asked them to carry a message to Salim, Ali's brother, and let him know that we were back in town, and then drove toward our apartment. We finally arrived about thirty minutes later, totally exhausted from the trip. We parked the car outside the iron gate and climbed the stairs to the second floor.

Mahji was relieved to see us and had some rice and lamb mixture to eat for dinner. As Mahji heated the dinner on her stove, Ali briefly related our adventures to her in Urdu. Ali had told her that he believed we would return sometime on Wednesday evening and to wait for us. We had made pretty good time on the road so we were home on Wednesday evening as predicted. That night each of us slept well because we were worn out from the long drive. It had been an interesting trip, but fast, and I wished we could have seen more of the Punjabi country side. Ali was worried about bandits and the possibility of robbery or even worse, so we made the drive as quickly as possible for safety's sake.

We rested for a few days at home and planned our weekend. This Saturday was Basant, the famous kite flying festival, and we would go to the old walled city to watch Babur and his younger brothers fly kites. The festival is supposed to mark the beginning of spring with the flying of all types, colors, and sizes of kites. The entire male population of Lahore participates in kite flying matches or "fights" to celebrate the coming of spring. Yellow is the main color in this event as it depicts the blossoming spring flowers in the fields of Punjab. People wear yellow cloths and fly yellow kites with yellow streamers attached to the tail to celebrate the holiday.

On Saturday we drove to the old walled city and parked the car in a parking area near the Bahti Gate. Ali and I walked to his brother's home and were welcomed by everyone in the neighborhood as we made our way through the alleys. The front door was a large double door made of heavy wood with a bolt and huge lock hanging on the front iron rings. It was unlocked because the family expected us to be arriving very soon. All eleven children were gathered in Salim's house, and his wife, Bahji, kissed my cheek and asked me to sit in the living room as we entered the front door. She immediately turned around and screamed shrilly at little Fozia to bring hot tea and sweet cakes from the kitchen. Bahji was a large, heavy woman, probably about 300 pounds, with a rather pinched and mean looking face. She had been given to Salim in an arranged marriage over seventeen years ago and was now the unchallenged mistress of his house. Seventeen years ago she was probably as pretty and petite as her only daughter, Fozia, now appeared. Her production of ten sons and one daughter solidified her place in the family. Several times I had heard Ali talk about how rough and harsh she was toward the children and Salim, but he never left her or even asked for a second wife, as was his right. Salim worked in a government office and made good money for his family. I heard later that he was given several promotions and was moving up the ladder in food procurement for the country of Pakistan.

Fozia was the only daughter of the family and was treated almost like a servant. She was a beautiful young girl of ten or eleven, with white, perfect teeth, and jet black hair flowing to her waist in a long braid. Woven in the braid was a strand of yellow material tied with a knot at the end. She was also wearing a loose fitting yellow chemise and pants outfit. She immediately ran to the kitchen and brought out a tray with tea cups and tea pot so we could sit down and relax. The living room was a room they usually kept closed off from the rest of the house with a locked door. The heavy lock was open now and we were shown in and told to sit on a plastic covered sofa. There were side tables that Fozia set the tray of tea and cakes upon so we could have our refreshments. Cousins who lived nearby knew I was coming to visit and soon began to slowly filter into the house. The women would shyly creep in and stare at me and then go to the kitchen or back bedroom to be away from the men. Fozia would stand near the side of the sofa and keep her head bowed, staring at the floor. When she thought I wasn't looking she would glance at me quickly. We immediately formed a strange bond of sorts. I felt sorry for this slim, overworked girl child, and she was dazzled by the young American woman married to her uncle. I always tried to be especially attentive to Fozia during my stay in Pakistan because I knew her mother treated her badly and her brothers were always teasing her. If I could give her a tiny feeling of being special I would try my best to do so. But every time I paid any attention to Fozia her mother would get a dark look on her face and snap some order to her in a harsh voice. Fozia would then run from the room and hasten to carry out the order before she was beaten for slowness. I decided to do my good deeds out of ear or eye shot of Bahji, Fozia's not-so-kind mother.

Basant is not only a kite flying event, but also a cultural festival of traditional food, dresses, dances, and music. For twenty-four hours thousands of multi-colored kites fill the skies, their elegant flight picked out even during the night by large spot lights. This is no ordinary kite flying, because most participants use string which has been coated by hand in a doughy substance impregnated with pulverized glass. This makes it easy for kites to fight in the air, and the most skilled or luckiest flyers can cut the string of their opponents and watch the lost kite flutter to the ground. Most kite flyers look for many kite fights and easily steer their kites into the path of others, and, with the flick of a wrist, try to cut them down. This festival is a tradition of the Punjab region, pre-dating the partition and creation of Pakistan.

The Muslim clerics see the festival as un-Islamic and pagan, not just because it encourages immodest behavior, but because it is celebrated by Sikhs and Hindus as well as Muslims. The Muslim religious "right wing" is not pleased at all by this festival and calls it a "sell-out" to Western values and ambitions. Even though it is rather unruly, Basant continues as a favorite holiday in Lahore and hopefully will not be outlawed.

There is a dark side to Basant. Every year young people are killed, either by falling from buildings or by walking into the paths of cars while flying kites or just gazing at them in the sky. There are often stories of young children being caught in a stray glass-covered sharp string and having their throats cut. Some rogue kite flyers might use wire instead of string and that makes life even more dangerous, for kite wires have been caught in electrical wires and sent bolts of electricity to instantly kill a man or boy. Most of the kite battles take place in the old walled city of Lahore. Boys and men gather on roof tops and fly their kites in fierce battles across large expanses of space between the houses.

Here we were in the midst of Basant, in the old walled city visiting my brother-in-law's home. I begged to be taken to the roof to see some of the kite battles. Babur, the oldest nephew, led me up the winding narrow stair case to the roof of their three story home. I was amazed at the sight spread out before me from the roof. A million roofs with over two million colorful kites engaged in battles over our heads, cheering boys with rags tied around their hands to keep from bleeding where the glass covered string had cut them. Music was playing from radios and phonographs placed in windows and on surrounding roof tops blasted in our ears.

I watched Babur and Sikandar, his younger brother, engage in a battle with their neighbor. Babur won this contest by cutting the kite string of his opponent with the flick of his wrist and immediately moving toward another kite to try and catch it also. Of course, I ask if I could fly a kite, too, but was immediately warned that women did not have kite battles with anyone. Women were supposed to watch from the sideline and cheer on their brothers, husbands, or fathers during this festival.

Out of the corner of my eye I saw Fozia standing at the open doorway to the roof. She also wanted to fly a kite, but she knew that if she asked she would be beaten by her brothers and sent back down the stairs to work in the kitchen. I beckoned for her to come out on the roof and stand by me to watch the festival. She inched out toward me and then ran to grab me around the waist and hold me tightly. Her brothers screamed at her, but she reached me quickly and I protected her from their angry gestures. Fozia was supposed to be working and not enjoying herself all day. It was only because I was there protecting her that she was able to have a few minutes break from her chores. I knew her older brothers were screaming orders to her in Urdu to leave me alone and return to her work in the kitchen. It is interesting that they enjoyed being with me and speaking English, but Fozia could not have the same freedom with her own Aunt Leila.

That evening, after a dinner of lamb, yogurt, and rice eaten on the small coffee table in Salim's living room, Ali, Mahji, and I drove home in the Volkswagen. I asked Ali if Fozia could come and stay with us for awhile to help Mahji with the chores around the house. Ali said that he would ask Fozia's father, Salim, but he doubted that Bahji would allow her daughter to do anything more than short visits. I would see if I could help Fozia get out of her house a few more times during my stay in Pakistan, if only so that she would have some happy memories before she was married off to a cousin or business partner of her father's and made to work in her husband's house instead of her parents' home.

The role of girls and women in Muslim countries is very harsh unless they are from wealthy families, and even then they are still controlled by men. I had heard many stories and even met some of the women trapped in these arranged marriages. Young women were basically raped by their new husbands, not given any freedoms or education, kept in seclusion with their girl children, and were not allowed to own property. Their husbands control any wealth they might have from their birth families, and if the women are unhappy or wish to leave they are beaten by members of the marriage family such as their husband, his brother, or father for not being submissive. Many young girls are put into arranged marriages with much older men. Muslim countries did not have any laws about how old a girl must be to be married, and when pushed to outlaw child marriages, the majority of Muslim countries objected. The Qur'an has verses that talk about how wonderful it is for Muslim men to have a child bride, one who has not even started to menstruate yet, so they can have sex any time they wish with the poor girl.

Possibly in the year 650 AD, when Mohammed was alive, this practice of marriage to children might have been something that was culturally necessary, but I began to see young girls married in 1969 Pakistan at a very young age also. The only thing that saves these young women are families that are educated and try to understand the pain and anguish they are subjecting their young daughters to by arranging a marriage with a man who is not suitable for her. Compassion is not something that is recognized as being a virtue in Pakistani society.

One day at a party, I approached a group of Ali's male friends who were laughing and talking about one of their acquaintances. I asked Ali what the joke was all about and he told me that one of the men had recently gotten married and was so wild when having constant sex with his new wife that after several months the violent sex caused her to have a miscarriage. Ali and his friends took this as a sign that their friend was very virile and quite the lover. They found the story funny and had no sympathy for the poor woman involved.

I didn't understand the joke and believed it to be one more indication that Pakistani society cares only for the pleasure of men, and has no regard for the feelings of women. To these men sex was only for the pleasure and sport of the man involved – the pain experienced by the woman did not matter to them at all and was considered a joke. This man did not love his wife. He hardly knew her when they were married because it was an arranged marriage. She was probably terrified and lonely; she was separated from her own family immediately after her wedding. He brutally chased her from room to room in their new home and raped her repeatedly until she was finally allowed to visit her mother and father when she had a miscarriage of her first pregnancy.

CHAPTER 7: WORKING FOR THE AMERICANS

During the Embassy tea party several months before, one of the American women mentioned to me that the Lahore American School often had job openings for American workers. When I repeated this information to Ali, he enthusiastically said I should apply for a job to make a little extra money to spend on souvenirs I wanted to take back to America. Now that we had our Volkswagen, he could drop me off at the school before going to his university job and pick me up later. The Lahore American School was located inside the compound near the American Consulate. It had been founded in 1956 and housed grade levels from nursery school through high school. Ali took me there one day to inquire about jobs at the school administration. I walked into an imposing building that resembled a high school in any town in America. There was a list of jobs posted on the main bulletin board in the front hallway of the school. A secretary in the school administration told me to just fill out an application form and leave it with her. At that time there happened to be a part time "Library Assistant" job open. I filled out the job application and gave it to the secretary in the office. Ali and I then left and he dropped me back at the home while he proceeded on to his job at the university.

Within a few days I received a hand written note delivered by a driver from the school. The note was from the librarian asking me to come speak with her about the job opening. On the day of the interview Ali drove me to the American School and I walked in the front door alone while he waited outside in the car until my interview with the librarian was finished. The school is a large two story building with many classrooms and a beautiful library. There is even a cafeteria which serves American food to the students. It resembles any school in the United States except that the architecture is similar to other large Pakistani buildings in Lahore. Desks, chairs, and bookcases, made in America, were throughout the entire building in classrooms, in the library, in study hall, and other rooms. Walking down the hallways I noticed that each classroom was equipped as classrooms in the United States might have been with age appropriate equipment for the teachers to use. All of the teachers seemed to be American citizens and most of them were wives of men who worked at the embassy. It was as if I had stepped into a school in the United States and not in Lahore, Pakistan.

Later in my stay in Pakistan I would be able to compare the American School to a girls' school in Lahore and understand how poorly Pakistan runs and equips its own schools. Women are especially discriminated against in the area of education. Most women decide not to attend school past about 10th grade if they are even lucky enough to go that far in the educational system. Much of their education is Islamic during these years, but they are given some reading, writing, and math.

I informed the administrative secretary that I was there to interview with the librarian and she escorted me up the steps to the second floor and showed me where the library was located. I walked into a large room with walls lined by shelves of all types of books. In the middle of the room sat a woman of about fifty years of age at a wooden desk, obviously the librarian. Introducing myself, we began to talk for awhile about my past experience in the library at Southern Illinois University. Of course, I told her why I was in Pakistan and she commented on the Pakistani clothes that I was wearing. She did not make negative remarks on my marriage to a man from Lahore, but did not smile or say anything positive about it, either. The librarian wanted someone who could shelve books on Mondays, Wednesdays, and Fridays of each week and only for four hours per day. That was not much work, but perfect for me, because it paid approximately $200 per month and there were only two months left until the end of school. That money would allow me to begin buying items in Pakistan that I might want to carry home to relatives or for myself. She offered me the job while I was sitting there and I accepted immediately. My past experience working in a library must have impressed her or maybe she just did not have anyone else to do the work. I was to start work at the school the following Monday morning.

When I informed Ali about the job offer, he was excited. His first response was to ask if pay checks were in American dollars or Pakistani rupees. It never crossed my mind to ask that question in the interview, but I really did not care until Ali told me I could be receiving twice the exchange rate for American dollars if I cashed the check and gave the money to him so he could go to the black market to exchange the dollars into rupees. There was a black market in American dollars and Ali assured me he knew certain people in Lahore. The way he explained it was that he could sell American dollars to Pakistani mafia members for a much higher amount than you could get paid at the American bank where I cashed my pay check. My eyes got pretty large as I realized that I could get double my pay check by just allowing Ali to take the money and bring me back rupees. I told Ali that I would ask next week when I filled out the employment papers and started working. I really did not realize that the black market in American dollars was illegal. It seemed fine to me to make the most of the money I would be earning from the American School even though I suspected that it was frowned upon.

I arrived at the American School the following Monday morning at 8:00 o'clock and immediately the administrative secretary gave some basic employment papers to fill out before starting work. It was simple paperwork such as my name, address, social security number, etc. I took the opportunity to ask the secretary about the method of payment and if I would receive dollars or rupees for my work. The secretary said I could have what I wished and if I wanted dollars to just indicate it on my employment paperwork. I finished the paperwork and immediately went to report to the librarian. In the library I was given a quick tour of the book shelves and the librarian explained to me what she wished done while I was there. It was simple filing and book shelving according to the Dewey Decimal System. The work was designed to get the library in order and books off of the librarians' desk where they accumulated during the day. I was also supposed to review the shelves and find books and magazines that children had left laying around the area. It was an extremely simple job and could have been done by one of the older students, but was not offered to the children in the school.

I started working on the piles of books stacked on a library cart and immediately got the idea of the library lay out. Moving through the long book stacks I straightened and re-shelved children's books and various periodicals that had been briefly used and discarded on the tables and chairs. Time passed quickly and around noon I said goodbye, wrote my time down on a time sheet and indicated I would return on Wednesday. Ali was waiting outside in the Volkswagen to take me home.

He had arranged his classes at the university so that he could drop me off and pick me up at the American School on the days that I would work. I told him that my check would be in American dollars and a big smile appeared on his face. I would receive my first check at the end of the month.

For several weeks I worked at the American School every Monday, Wednesday, and Friday morning. Several times I would bring my lunch because Ali could not pick me up as promptly as he had earlier estimated. On these days after my shift in the library, I would have the opportunity to sit with several of the American teachers and talk for a few minutes while we finished our lunches. During one of these chat sessions an interesting story about an English girl named Nancy was being discussed. Six years ago Nancy had met her husband, a Shiite Muslim named Hussein, in England and they had fallen in love and married. She accompanied him to Pakistan where she lived with his entire family in a large multi-house compound. What she did not know about her husband before she married him was that he was the second oldest son of a family which was part of the Shia aristocracy or directly descended from a Caliph that lived in the 9th century. The family had sent their son to England to be educated but did not really want him to marry an English girl. This marriage was an ill conceived plan done without an understanding of the culture by Nancy and a complete lack of concern by Hussein for Nancy's future welfare. Nancy did convert to Islam and for a while acted as the perfect Muslim wife to Hussein. She became pregnant and produced a wonderful son for the family to adore. She spoke Urdu correctly and lived as a Shiite Muslim girl in Pakistan, even wearing the veil or burkah when she ventured out in society.

After several years she wished to return to England to visit grandparents and other family members and to take her son with her so that they could get to know their grandson. Hussein's parents disagreed and the family began to fight with Nancy. She was ultimately thrown out of the family compound and not given any access to her young son or even her husband. Finally his family forced him to divorce Nancy and they arranged a marriage for him to a young Shiite Pakistani girl. Nancy was heartbroken and depressed. She continued to live in an apartment in Lahore, worked in the American School, and prayed to see her son again someday. In Islamic and Pakistani law the children are the sole property of the husband. No wife has any legal control over what happens to her own children, especially if the children are male. If this young child had been a girl, things might have been a little different for Nancy; she might have been able to take a daughter to England to visit grandparents. In fact, if she had stolen a daughter and taken her to England, the Shiite family would not have cared much. A girl child is usually considered a burden to a family and not a joy.

But because the child was a boy, the Shiite family linage created problems beyond Nancy's understanding. Even though she had hired a local solicitor and taken the case to court in Lahore, she had not estimated the ability of this particular family to keep her son from her. This young boy, with his English mother, was a direct descendant of a Shiite Caliph. He would be brought up in the Shiite religion, educated in this backward country, and marry whoever the family patriarch told him to marry. This small child would probably never be able to see his English mother again in his life. She would always be looking for ways to visit her beloved son while she lived and worked in Pakistan to support herself. Her husband's family would be in total control of the boy's life and education, and I am sure they told him terrible lies about Nancy as he got older.

The American women told me that during this last Tenth of Muhjarram, which I had witnessed earlier in the year, Nancy's husband and son were the man and boy holding the reins of the pure white Arabian stallion leading the procession of the faithful shouting "Imam Husain" while beating themselves. Of course, the small boy, Nancy's son, was only about four years old and had to be held on his father's shoulders. Hussein and the boy were completely clothed in black robes with black turbans on their heads. Their job was to manage the white horse leading the mob and make sure it was not hurt or somehow escaped from their control. Nancy had been able to rent a room above the street level where the procession was passing and view for a moment her young son as he passed with his father. This was the only view she could get of her son or husband since she has been thrown out of the family compound.

The story was heartbreaking and I felt, for a moment, this woman's loss of control over the one thing she loved more than any other in the world. American and British women are brought up to believe that they have some control over their own lives. In Pakistan and other Muslim countries woman have no control over any aspect of their lives or the lives of their children. Men are totally in control of everything that happens to women, and if they don't want you anymore, you will be gotten rid of fast.

When I told the story to Ali later that day, he said that she would never see her son again and that she should probably leave Pakistan and return to England. He also asked me to never mention this story about Nancy to his friend Shahji, who was a Shiite. No one had sympathy for Nancy and her grief, except other American and English women.

I was profoundly affected by Nancy's story and my shock that this country had laws that could separate a mother from her child so easily. It certainly gave me reasons to think about myself and any future children I might have. This was a good lesson for me to learn about the second class citizenship that women experience in Muslim countries.

At the end of the month I received my first pay check from the American School. The check was for approximately $200.00 and, on the legal exchange rate in rupees at that time, worth about seven rupees to one dollar. Therefore, this one check was valued at about fourteen hundred rupees. I believe that Ali was being paid about two thousand rupees per month from his university job, and for me to bring in so much additional money in one month was a big deal. The check was written in American dollars and so I took it to an American bank in Lahore and cashed it. Ali waited in the car outside the bank while I cashed the check. When I finally left the bank and got in our car, I immediately gave the American dollars to Ali to keep. He took me back to our home and left me there while he went down to the old walled city to find someone in the black market to change the money to rupees. After about four hours he returned home with over twenty-four hundred rupees that he had received for the dollars. I took half of the money and put it away for a shopping trip to the bazaar. Ali kept the other half for his savings account.

I only worked for the American School for two months. School was out in May and no one was employed until after the monsoon season was over. Appling for the job again in the fall semester I found out they had already hired another American girl, this one was not married to a Pakistani, but the daughter of one of the consulate staff. I had received one more paycheck of two hundred dollars and we did exactly the same procedure as with the first check. So now I had approximately two thousand rupees to spend on almost anything I wished. Ali had promised to take me shopping in the bazaar inside the old walled city. I could hardly wait for the chance, but I had to have Ali go with me, for protection, translation, and bargaining expertise.

Friday was the holy day of the Islamic week and men would flock to the mosques and pray most of the day. Ali never went to pray at a mosque and usually stayed home with me or we visited friends at their homes on this day. Sometimes we would visit his brother's family, but I tried to avoid going to the old walled city as much as possible. I would prefer to invite some of them to our house because the bathrooms were better and the sewers outside our house did not smell so badly. We decided to go shopping on a Saturday in late May because the weather was pleasant and the monsoons that would happen later in the summer could cause too much of a problem in the bazaars with running water down the open sewers in the old walled city.

We drove down town to the walled city and parked the car along the wall. Children immediately ran up to us and asked in Urdu to wash the car. Along the walls of the city would be maimed beggars, usually missing a leg or arm, sitting on dirty clothes while holding out a small dish or bowl with a few anas in it. Ali sent them scurrying with loud shouts and arm waves toward them. Twenty or thirty young, ragged children followed us with their hands out begging for anas, Pakistani coins which were worth less than a penny. Their voices whined ana, ana, ana, repeatedly in our ears as we hurriedly walked toward the Delhi Gate. This gate is an entrance on the eastern wall of the walled city, named because it faces the road toward Delhi. A very large bazaar is located inside this gate and this was where we were headed to shop for gold, silver, and cloth.

I was curious about the beggar children that had followed us outside the gate and Ali told me that they could be children of the red light district women. Some of the maimed beggars had either performed the painful injuries on themselves or to their own children so that they would be able to beg and receive more sympathy from passersby. He did not give them any money, even though we had plenty of anas in our pockets. He cautioned me not to taken in and give them money, saying it would encourage them in their begging activities. They looked so poor and sad that I was bothered that Ali would not allow me drop a few anas in their waiting hands. I had seen other people provide the beggars with some pocket change and afterward the children ran away and left them alone. It seemed selfish not to provide a small amount of money to these children who had so little in life. But Ali was adamant about the beggars, and he screamed at them to leave us alone while we headed toward the bazaar to go shopping.

After moving down some streets with small shops on each side, we reached the silver and gold jewelry bazaar. I was impressed with how much gold was in each man's small, square cubicle. I was looking for some small gold earrings for myself. The earrings that were given to me on my wedding day were much too large and heavy for me to wear. We sold the heavy earrings to Salim and therefore I was looking for something to replace them that could be worn every day. Ali and I walked down a row of shops filled with gold jewelry and finally stopped at one. We entered and sat down to look at the beautiful jewelry the shop keeper had to offer us. The shop keeper pulled out hundreds of gold bangles tied together in a bundle and put them on the velvet in front of me so that I could pick them up and look at each one. The gold was high karat with both twenty-two and twenty-four karat in the pile of bracelets. Each bracelet has a different design carved into the gold. Some had beautiful flowers, all of tinted gold with pink petals and red and green stained leaves. Other bracelets had swirls and wines carved into the bracelets. I was in heaven holding and feasting my eyes on so much gold. I had never seen stacks of bracelets, rings, earrings, and other jewelry items that Pakistani women wore. This was mostly wedding jewelry. A Pakistani woman took with her, as her dowry on her wedding day, thousands of dollars of pure gold jewelry. The richer the family was, the more jewelry a bride will wear to show the world what she brings to her new family   This dowry is extremely important and every bride must have something gold to wear on this most important day in her life. This is one of the reasons that girl children were not loved as much as boys. Each girl must be married someday, and with this marriage goes some of the wealth of the family. A boy child brings to his family a new bride and with the bride comes the wealth of their family. So a family with many sons receives all the gold and a family with many daughters eventually loses money. This is also why marriages are arranged in Pakistan. Each family wants to insure that any gold goes to other family members such as first and second cousins or business partners of the father. If the gold goes outside of the family it is not a happy day for the relatives. Marriage with cousins in Pakistan is the preferred connection, not at all frowned upon for genetic reasons or any other reasons. Sometimes marriages between wealthy business partners' children might be negotiated to keep the business together.

I carefully looked at the many earring styles that were shown to me by the shop keeper. I only wanted a simple, light weight earring that could be worn easily. Ali was upset about my choice because light weight gold was cheap and people would think he was poor. So I changed my choice to a heavier gold and got something that I ended up never wearing except at events or weddings I would attend in Pakistan. Many other items were shown to me, including the ornate earring and nose combination of rings that were attached to each other by chains. It was interesting to look at but too ornate, and I did not have a pierced nose, which was needed to wear this combination. Many brides were dressed in this style of jewelry, as I would later observe.

When we left the gold shop I spotted a silver market very close by and asked Ali if we could look at some of the silver jewelry. We entered a shop and in glass cases I viewed piles of silver belts, ankle bells, bracelets, necklaces, and other items. I asked specifically about a silver belt that was displayed. It was constructed in sections of ornately designed rings and silver balls. The idea was to put together as many sections of the belt as would fit around your waist. I wanted this belt, and we measured my waist and put together enough sections so that it would fit me. The belt was sold by weight, and after the entire item was hooked together it was put on a scale and weighed. I believe the entire belt cost the equivalent of about $25.00 or 175 rupees. I thought that was pretty cheap for an American to buy such heavy and beautifully crafted silver. I was told it was pure silver and not adulterated in any way, but I had no way of testing this statement and had to take their word for it.

We then made our way to the shawl market. Many stalls of beautifully embroidered wool Kashmiri shawls of various sizes were in each of the shops in this area. I was enchanted with the different colors and embroidery on each of the fine wool shawls. We entered a shop and began looking at hundreds of shawls. I finally settled upon a black wool shawl with red, rust, blue, and yellow embroidered flowers, a tan wool shawl with green, rust and brown embroidery, and a tan wool shawl with rust and gold embroidery on the borders. We paid about 70 rupees for each shawl after much bargaining by Ali in Urdu, about $10.00 in our currency. The shawls were wrapped up in newspaper and tied with a string.

We left that shop and continued down one of the streets, suddenly finding ourselves surrounded by shops with spices and tea spread out in barrels in front of each one. I could not believe the smells and colors that were before my eyes in this area of the bazaar. The spices were amazing to look at in all colors of the rainbow. Peppers, curry, flowers, nuts, cinnamon, cardamom, and many, many others that I could not recognize were in very large quantities. Barrels full of teas were spread out before us and each tea was a different color or texture. We decided to stock up on some of the herbs and teas to take with us back to the house. Ali chose several and each one was put in a cone of newspaper after it was weighed and priced. The end of the newspaper cone was then folded over to cover the tea or herb and given to us in a larger folded newspaper container wrapped with string to easily carry.

We had our arms full of purchases and headed toward the car outside the Delhi Gate. As we emerged from the gate to the concrete sidewalk, about fifteen beggar children headed for us and begin crying the word "anas" again. Ali just ignored their pleas and we walked toward the car to unload our burdens. At the car a man was cleaning our windshield and expected to be rewarded for taking care of the car while we were shopping in the Bazaar. Ali gave him a couple of anas and we then got into the car and drove off. We did not visit his relatives this trip, but headed back to our home in the suburbs of Lahore. Mahji would be making dinner for us and had asked us to bring some spinach home for her to use in the dinner. We had to stop at a vegetable stall to find some good spinach and Ali did the buying for us. I was not allowed to shop alone and could only do so with men to speak Urdu and perform any type of bargaining with the merchants. All women, except widows, usually had men do their grocery shopping for them. There were no grocery stores that I saw while I was in Lahore, only small shops or sellers of fresh and dried produce. Men would go out early in the day to purchase all the food for the evening meal in a variety of shops and bring it home for the women to prepare. You could buy imported items such as Turkish coffee or British Biscuits, but they were expensive and considered luxuries for almost everyone. I was not a coffee drinker at that time so I enjoyed many types of tea which were available because they were grown in the Himalayan mountain country of Pakistan, India, Nepal, and Kashmir.

Everyone drank hot tea or chai, usually mixed with milk and sugar. It was extremely good and I enjoyed it every morning and afternoon.

I had mentioned to Ali that I felt bad because Mahji was doing too much house work at her age and that we should hire a person to help her with whatever she needed. After thinking about it and talking to Mahji concerning what she wished, Ali said he would get her a young boy who could sweep and clean. He talked to Shahji, his friend, about where to find a young boy who needed work and could live at our house to help Mahji. After about one week a very young boy of about seven or eight years old was brought to our house by his father, a farmer from the country. The boy was dressed in new clothes and was a beautiful young child, with black hair, straight white teeth, and beautiful liquid dark eyes. This child held on to his father's leg and appeared to be very afraid of us all. After Ali and the father completed the negotiations about the boy and Ali gave him a few coins, the father left him at our house to live with us. Mahji immediately took charge of the child and had him working immediately sweeping the porch and stairs. The young boy was homesick and always had tears in his eyes. Mahji said that at night, when he slept in a char pi near her, he cried all the time. Mahji told us this in an irritated voice and I could tell that she was not happy with the young worker. I wondered how a family could give up such a young child and was told that they were a poor country family and needed the money the child would make in our service. I could not make friends with the boy; he was very afraid of me and would not come close or look at me. Mahji ordered him to sweep the floors, washed clothes and dishes for us. He would do it, but never smiled at us during his work. We fed him and gave him a place to sleep which was comfortable, but he missed his home.

After about two weeks Mahji and Ali could not stand it any longer and asked Shahji to take the boy home to his parents. When he heard he was going home his face lit up in a big smile. The few days he was with us we had never seen that smile or a laugh. I am sure his parents were disappointed that he did not work out as a servant, but he was still young. I always felt bad about the boy being taken from his parents whom he obviously loved and missed excessively. I never asked Ali for a servant again. I was not sure why they had not hired an older boy, or a young woman, except for possible reasons in finding a "moral" young woman. Boys had to be below the age of 13 for them to be left alone in a house with a pure Muslim woman like Mahji. So, because of her strict adherence to Islam, it was not easy to find a servant to help her. I also believe that Mahji did not want any young girls to help with the housework because Ali's nephews were in the house so often. I was never asked to help in any way around the house and could not cook for anyone. I asked Ali to buy me some ground beef one day, so that I could make hamburgers for us all for dinner. He said that beef was not very tasty in Pakistan and that I would be disappointed by it. But I begged and he relented and went to find ground beef so I could try making my own dinner. What he brought home looked all right, and was ground beef, but when I made hamburgers we all got ill with stomach problems. I mixed the meat with spices and onions just as I would have done in the states. We then fried the hamburgers on the small frying pan that Mahji had in the kitchen. When they were cooked all the way through we put the hamburgers on the flat wheat bread and tried to eat them. The beef taste was nothing like American beef. I guess Pakistani cows are not corn fed or grain fed and only Allah knows what they eat, but it tastes extremely bad. I never asked for beef again and grew to love the goat meat, lamb, and chicken recipes that Mahji made daily. I guess when in Pakistan there is good reason why you always must eat what the Pakistanis eat.

CHAPTER 8: THE GARDENS AT SHALIMAR

The Moghul Emperor Babur kept a diary his entire life and historians refer to it as the Babur-nama. Babur was the great, great, grandfather of the Emperor Shah Jahan. The Moghul Emperors loved gardens and Babur referred to them in his Babur-nama as "the purest of human pleasure." Shalimar Gardens is located on the Grand Trunk Road about seven miles out of Lahore toward the border with India. This garden was laid out by Shah Jahan in 1642 for the pleasure of his royal household, who often stayed for days or weeks in this imperial splendor. The word "Shalimar" means "house of joy" and the passing centuries have done nothing to detract from the majestic atmosphere of beauty and tranquility in forty-two acres of lavish fountains, lawns, flowers, and fruit trees. If you look closely, you might see the beautiful women of Shah Jahan's harem wandering as ghosts throughout this fairy tale setting.

A marble pavilion under which water flows and cascades over a carved marble slab creates a waterfall effect. Across the waterfall is a marble throne situated in the gleaming white pavilion. The emperor's sleeping quarters are at the center of the west wall, across from the public audience hall, which is located just outside of the garden. The emperor walked through this hall daily to show himself to his admiring public gathered in a separate walled garden outside. There are over four hundred fountains, surrounded by flower beds, fruit trees, shaded walks, ponds, and waterfalls in Shalimar.

We decided to take an afternoon trip to Shah Jahan's Shalimar gardens so that we could casually wander in the cool shade of a hot May afternoon. Ali made the request to his brother, Salim, that we take Fozia with us and also one of the younger children, instead of the older boys who might not appreciate the attention so much. Fozia had never seen the gardens and, of course, neither had I, so we were both excited to go. We decided to also take five year old Khurram, the youngest of Salim's sons, to let him run on the beautiful green lawns. Khurram and Fozia had grown up in the squalor of the old walled city and I don't believe they got out often to see beautiful things. They were both excited to visit the gardens with their Uncle Ali and their American Aunt Layla. We made a picnic lunch of boiled eggs, rice and roti (bread), and tea to take along and eat in the gardens. I decided to wear a flowered orange sari which was light weight, and some small comfortable sandals. The weather in May brings the hot weather to Lahore, and even though it is located at a higher altitude, by this time of year we needed a cool place to visit. Temperatures during the day can reach ninety degrees or higher in May, so the lifestyle of the local population begins to slow down in this month.

I had heard about Shalimar and wanted to feel as if we had moved back in time and was walking in the Emperor's garden with his harem instead of a historical ruin in modern day Lahore. We drove out of Lahore toward the border with India about 7 or 8 miles along a tree lined road toward

Shalimar Gardens. Other Pakistani visitors were at the gardens also and we had to park along the road, get out of the car, and walk into the front gate. It was just as if we had suddenly gone back in time three hundred years. As we emerged into the huge lawn with fountains and flowers, I was amazed at the beauty surrounding us. Little Khurram wouldn't hold my hand any longer and wanted to run and roll on the lawn. It was probably the first time he had seen anything like this garden before in his short life. Fozia acted exactly the opposite and was shy while she walked with me holding my hand with both of hers so that she could be near me the entire time. I only knew a few words of Urdu and could speak in very short sentences to Fozia. She knew no English at all and was extremely quiet around me.

Ali carried the picnic lunch and we walked around viewing the interesting fountains and various gardens. Ali kept his eyes on little Khurram because it would be easy for him to get lost in these gardens. Every now and then he would call something in Urdu to Khurram and the child would run back to our sides to try and behave for a moment before he ran off again to play. I believe Khurram was in heaven for this short afternoon.

We ate our lunch on the lawn under a tree and watched as the fountains sprayed their streams of water high in the air. A canal runs the entire 2006 foot length of the gardens and from its four hundred sparkling fountains shoot up skeins of fresh water that cools and refreshes the air. It was a magical afternoon that I think about occasionally these days, forty years later. It was magical because of its location and the fascinating history behind the beauty of the creations of Moghul India. The day was heavenly and we all enjoyed our visit to such a beautiful place, but we had to leave and take the children back to their home in the old walled city.

Walking through the old walled city can make you all the more conscious of the transition from heavenly garden to filthy open sewers and spicy smells of current day Lahore. I am glad we had a few moments to take the children out of their day to day environment and show them the beautiful Shalimar Gardens. We returned the children to their parents, stayed a few minutes for a cup of tea, and drove back to our own apartment thinking of the beautiful day we had experienced.

May was the beginning of the hot weather in Lahore and the consequences of this weather to many citizens seemed to be stomach illness of every kind. I had been careful to avoid food and water that I thought might cause me to be sick, but despite these avoidance tactics I acquired a very violent intestinal illness. I was too weak to leave the bed and Ali had to hold me up and help me to the bathroom every time I needed to vomit or have diarrhea. The whole house was worried about me because the only thing I could do was drink tea and moan in bed. I was miserable with this illness. Immediately upon viewing my distress, Ali's mother, Mahji went to her kitchen and concocted a brew of tea and herbs. The mixture was extremely strong and I could only drink small amounts of it, but Mahji kept bringing it to me. The tea had a strong taste of licorice, but I believe there was some cinnamon, cardamom, and chamomile in it also. The recipe was a secret one passed down for many generations in her family, of course.

The poor population in Pakistan could not afford drugs from drug stores, and before the British brought western medicine to India there were many effective ways of curing most local diseases. Every household had herbal remedies that work for their own native diseases and maladies. Sure enough, the tea cured me and I was up and about in two days. For a few days afterwards I could only eat brown rice and boiled eggs, but soon I was back to having the same delicious foods that everyone else was eating, minus the hot spices. I only got ill about three times in Lahore and it was always the same illness with the same symptoms. Mahji cured me every time with her medicinal licorice tea.

I lost about ten pounds during my stay in Pakistan, mainly due the fact that I was rarely eating any types of fatty or sweetened foods that we Americans call junk foods. All of our food was cooked fresh everyday and with unprocessed ingredients. We only used sugar for our tea and it was unrefined sugar in large brownish chunks rather than small white crystals. The cakes and sweet candy that you could buy at the local bakery were all too sweet for me to eat so I never indulged in them. Mahji cooked everything in "ghee" or clarified butter. She usually purchased this ghee from a local vender. Ghee does not need to be refrigerated and can keep for over a month in a closed container. Gee is made by slowly cooking pure butter until it separates from its milk solids. The cooled substance has the foam scraped off the top and is filtered through cheesecloth to retain the 100% butterfat. Pakistanis love the taste of ghee and use it on all bread, rice, and to fry meat and vegetables. I could never get used to the taste of ghee straight and everyone in the family thought I was strange because of my inability to put it on bread or other food. I much preferred plain yogurt for my rice and some jam for my toast. I didn't mind ghee used in fried foods and one of my favorite dishes was lentil cakes that were fried on a little iron skillet. I would beg Mahji to cook them for me, and once she showed me how to do it. She would boil the lentils for an hour until they were soft and then let them cool. She would then grind them up into a kind of flour, add water, and then form a small, flat, disk with a few spices such as parsley and onions mixed into the batter. She then hand formed flat patties and put them into the frying pan with ghee to fry. They were delicious, and I ate them whenever she would take the time to make them for me.

I never took antibiotics in Pakistan because other than the stomach problems I did not get sick, not even a cold. However, anyone could visit a pharmacy and purchase either locally made penicillin or the very expensive imported types of antibiotics from England without a doctor's prescription. There were factories in Pakistan that made some pharmaceutical items, but they were known for not being pure. One time while we were at the movies, there was a short subject film before the feature about a woman who died from polluted drugs made in Pakistan. It was supposed to put pressure on drug manufacturing firms to be careful with their ingredients. Apparently the government did not inspect these companies or have any regulations concerning their safe operations. They depended upon the free economy to force companies into safe operations. I suppose the government believed that if customers died or got sick using bad products, then the company would go bankrupt. Not a healthy way to enforce quality control in big Pakistani corporations.

It was late May and I was running low on my birth control pills. I did not want to have any children in this country and asked Ali to find out how to get a new supply. Ali had many friends and one of them was a physician. His name was Dr. Mohammed Rashid and he was approximately thirty-five years old. Dr. Rashid had been a friend of Ali's for many years and his family was what I would call upper middle class. One day we drove to Dr. Rashid's clinic in another part of Lahore and he supplied me with as many birth control pills as I would need for the next six months. There was a general push by some health groups in Pakistan to encourage women to plan their family sizes. The real problem was that most men did not want family planning for sons; only if their wives had daughters was it necessary. Birth control pills were not expensive and were manufactured in western countries, not in Pakistan, so you knew you were getting the real thing.

About a month later Ali said we were going to have tea with Dr. Rashid and a friend of his whom he wanted us to meet. We drove to his clinic and found him with a young twenty year old woman. The woman was a student in a local girl's college and had come to him for birth control pills sometime in the past. The girl's name was Sonia and she was not married, and very pretty. He had started to date her in secret and now was having a love affair with her. In fact, she was pregnant by him and needed an abortion. The problem was that if either one of them were caught by either family they would be in real trouble. Dr. Rashid was not married yet, but his mother had great plans for him and if he married anyone except whom his mother picked out for him she would disinherit him and he would suffer humiliation. He had no choice but to stop seeing Miss Sonia, arrange and pay for her abortion, and then marry whoever his parents had picked out for him.

Abortions in Pakistan were illegal and difficult to have performed by a doctor. Of course, because Dr. Rashid was a physician he could arrange one, but with great difficulty and it had to be done in secret. Sonia was a beautiful girl, but not of the same social status as Dr. Rashid. He had obviously taken advantage of her vulnerability and now was going to stop seeing her.

I felt rather irritated with the whole situation and began to understand the problems they might have if their secret was told to anyone. He had declared his affair to Ali because of their many years of friendship, and I suspect men have few people they can tell this type of story to in Pakistan. Fornication is a crime in Pakistan and most Muslim countries. The worst punishment for the crime of fornication is for the woman to suffer. A woman can spend time in prison if caught by police and Dr. Rashid could lose his physician's license. If she was discovered by her family even if they kept her secret, she would never be able to be married to anyone because she was no longer a virgin. She would be an outcast and probably would have difficulty making any type of living for herself in the future. Her future was pretty bleak now because she had been seduced by this doctor. Her only hope at a normal life was to keep the entire story secret and never tell anyone what had happened to her.

The abortion was performed a few weeks later in a neighboring town. Dr. Rashid paid a high price to have it done and made sure that Sonia was healthy before she returned to her studies at the girls' college. I don't know what story she used for her absence, but somehow she was not caught. I also don't know if Dr. Rashid ever saw Sonia again or continued to use her as he wished. He was the only person who knew her background and could have blackmailed her for many years. I do know that approximately three months after this incident we received an invitation to his wedding. His mother and father were marrying him to his second cousin, a much younger girl. The wedding ceremony was set for only a few weeks away.

We attended the wedding on a Saturday afternoon in late June 1969. Ali drove us to the groom's parents' house which turned out to be a large home on the outskirts of Lahore. Tents were placed around the outside of the house so that men and women could eat and watch the entertainment away from each other's sight.

I wore a blue sari with gold trim and all of my twenty-two karat gold jewelry to the wedding. I immediately separated from Ali and went to the women's tent to meet the bride. She was seated on a decorated bed, surrounded by her female family and friends. The bride was dressed entirely in red and gold. She appeared to be approximately sixteen years old to me. Her long black hair was braided with gold ribbons and a red and gold scarf was draped over her bowed head. She wore pounds of gold jewelry including rings on each finger and about twenty gold bangles stacked closely up each of her arms. She kept her eyes on the floor and would not say anything to me even though I greeted her in the traditional "Salaam Al Akum". She was extremely shy and seemed to be nervous about being married to Dr. Rashid. I believe she had met her new husband once before this wedding because they were distantly related. I have no doubt that she was a virgin and all of this activity was upsetting to her.

The match was a good one for her family and even though Dr. Rashid was at least twenty years older than she, everyone on both sides of the family was happy about the arranged marriage. This marriage was not a love match between the two newlyweds, but the bride had no choice in this wedding and had to make the most of it. Their families had decided there was to be a wedding and that was all that was needed. I am sure, even though she was afraid, she knew that this was the best opportunity that would be available to her. No one would ever tell her about her husband's indiscretions with the beautiful Sonia or how he set up and performed an illegal abortion to get rid of his own child. She would go through life believing her husband was an honest, moral member of the community. I suppose that naïve belief was best for them both in order to live a contented life in Pakistani society.

After spending some time with the bride and other women I went into the other tent to talk to Ali. He was speaking to some of the men and as I approached he smiled and introduced me to them. They were all friendly and, of course, spoke English well; after all, Dr. Rashid was extremely well educated and so were his friends. I don't remember ever speaking to Dr. Rashid again or even being invited to his home after the wedding. I guess we knew too much about his love life to be trusted for long with his new wife.

The entertainment was getting ready to begin and the men all pulled me to the front of the seated guests. A large circle of men formed around the musicians and began calling for them to start playing their music. There were six men who played drums, string instruments, cymbals, flutes, and rang bells. In the midst of the men stood one woman dressed in a green and gold short top, showing her stomach and baggie silk pants with a row of bells tied to her ankles. Her feet were bare and her finger and toe nails painted bright red. She had a long black braid hanging down her back and woven in the braid were gold tassels which sparkled. As the musicians began to play the woman raised her hands in front of her eyes, while looking through her fingers, and started to sing a high pitched song. The men stared at her because she was a professional dancing girl and of dubious character. Anyone could rent these entertainers from the old city and have them sing and dance at a feast or wedding. The women of the wedding party stood behind the walls of the women's tent and looked out through a mesh curtain. I was the only woman in the room allowed to sit in the front row and watch this professional dancer.

The dancer started to whirl around and stamp her feet to the beat of the music. Every time she stamped her feet the bells tied to her ankles would ring and the beat of the drums would match her feet. She sang a love song to the groom and whirled and twirled in an intricate dance step that was very Pakistani. I had seen a few movies by this time and this woman reminded me of the actresses in the Pakistani movies. The drums beat a fast tune while the musicians backed her up singing the song. It was a lively tune, and she moved quite seductively around the circle on the floor that the guests made for her. I was seated next to Ali on the floor watching the dancing girl intently. She noticed me almost immediately and her next song was directed toward me. I have no idea what she sang, but as she whirled and danced nearer and nearer to me, she looked directly into my eyes. I was forced to look down because of the intensity of her stare during this dance. I was blushing and wondering why she chose me to stare at, although I am sure it was because I was the foreigner. Her look confused me and I wondered if she was daring me to try and do the same dancing as she was doing. Of course, I could not dance and even if I could have, would not have done so at this celebration. Wedding guests don't dance with each other or by themselves at a Pakistani wedding. The entertainment was considered pretty risqué and the men were laughing about the attention paid to me by this dancer. I supposed I was being made fun of during her dance because all of her stares and gestures were directed at me. I had no idea what she was singing and the music was too loud to hear Ali's translation. It embarrassed me considerably and I turned away from her looks and ignored her song. She was a very good dancer and rather pretty, but not beautiful. I asked Ali about her and he told me she was from the old walled city red light district.

After about thirty-five minutes of dancing and singing the entertainment stopped and we all got up to go eat. A huge banquet was spread out on a very long table where the guests could feast on many sweets, a variety of rice dishes, lamb, chicken and other delights. The men picked up plates and walked along a side of the table first while the woman waited. After the men had left the food table and sat down at other tables away from the food, the woman were called into the room to eat. They took their full plates back into the bride's quarters to eat there. The bride did not eat anything that I could see at this party. Later that night Dr. Rashid would take his bride to his bedroom in the main house and consummate the marriage. The next morning his mother and the mother of the bride would inspect the sheets of the wedding bed to make sure the girl had been a virgin. I'm sure everything went well for the groom, but not so sure about the young bride's comfort. She seemed pretty unhappy about the whole thing. Maybe she would adjust over time and be content with her husband. For her sake, I hope she was able to learn to care for Dr. Rashid.

We returned home late that night and Ali told Mahji about the entire proceedings. She rarely went out to any event. Her evenings were spent praying on her red prayer rug in the corner of her bedroom.

Several times I watched Mahji prepare Fozia's long black hair. Fozia would sit in front of her grandmother on the floor and Mahji would put oil of some kind in her hair. I believe it was a vegetable oil or possibly olive oil that was used. She would then comb it through carefully until her waist length hair was coated with oil. Mahji would then begin to braid the hair tightly. I saw Fozia flinch a few times during the project of having her hair braided. When Mahji got a few inches down the braid, she would add a colored cloth or ribbon divided into three strands and begin to braid the cloth with every cross over of the hair. By the time she got to Fozia's waist, her hair and the cloth were tightly braided together and a small tassel would be hanging from the end of the braid. Sometimes the tassel would have a bell or other ornament attached to the end and this would flip around as Fozia tossed her head with every step. Mahji would oil her own salt and pepper colored hair too and braid it herself. Of course, she never put any colored cloth in her own hair; after all, she was an old widow and did not need adornment.

If Mahji washed her hair I never saw any shampoo, just the oil she used afterward and I think she might have used bar soap on it in the shower. Occasionally I saw her sitting up on the roof in a char pi with her wet hair spread out around her to dry after a shower. Her comb was a wooden one, approximately four inches long and saturated with oil. She had used this comb for years to finish her hair with oil every day. Most Pakistani women used oil on their hair, but not all of them. I would occasionally see women with clean, smooth un-oiled hair. The boys oiled their jet black hair also, and it looked like Elvis Presley's coiffure with the waves and grease. You had to be careful of where they put their heads on the furniture with so much oil in their coiffeurs. I always recoiled at the thought of touching their hair. Your hand would come away from their head coated with oil if you touched them. I was told that it kept their hair healthy, and maybe that was true, but I never had the desire to oil my own hair to match theirs.

One afternoon Mahji and I were home alone. I was reading a book in the bedroom and Mahji was in her room saying her prayer beads while sitting on her small rug. I happened to notice through the window that it was getting a little darker outside than was normal for about 3:00 o'clock in the afternoon. So, thinking it was going to rain, I went through the house to the front porch to look at the sky. The sky appeared a funny yellow color and the wind was beginning to blow trash around on the street. Everything appeared very strange to me so I went up to the roof to get a better look at the sky. As I walked out on the roof I turned to the west and was surprised to see a black wall of clouds extending from the horizon far up in the sky and it was slowly moving toward us. As I wondered if this was just a huge rain storm coming toward us, Babur came bursting into the house and rushed up the stairs to the roof. He screamed at me to immediately get to the rooms below and help him close the windows and doors. I pointed toward the horizon and asked him what was in the storm moving toward us. He immediately shouted that it was a terrible dust storm and if we did not prepare the house we would be sorry afterward. Obviously, the dust storm was moving fairly fast in our direction, so we ran down the steps and started locking all of the windows that had been open because of the hot weather. Mahji took one look out the window and began stuffing towels and rags under the doors.

Having sealed the house as best we could we all sat in the living room, the one room in the house without windows, and awaited the storm. Mahji brought me a heavy cloth to wrap around my mouth and nose and I watched Babur do the same with a towel. Within ten minutes the storm hit our house with a sudden blast of wind and dust. It blew fiercely for at least an hour, driving dust in every existing crack under the doors and around the windows. You could see dust hanging in the air of the living room and taste grit in your mouth. The wind howled with a loud growling noise and I was afraid that the windows would break under the pressure. Dust was everywhere in the house and in our eyes, noses, and ears. My hair was gritty with dust and dirt blown around by the storm. We sat waiting for the storm to end and probably even praying a little during the worst part of the tempest.

Finally the storm moved away from us and we got up to see what damage had been done. The house and furniture were all a dusty brown color and there was a thick layer on all inside floors. When we opened the door to go out on the small porch we were surprised at the depth of the dust. It was at least six inches deep in places on the porch and in front of the bathroom doors on the stairway. You could barely walk down the stairs because the dust had accumulated in drifts on each step.

The clean-up process was a huge amount of work for all of us to accomplish. Mahji began sweeping with a hand broom while Babur carried buckets of dust down the stairs to the street and dumped them. I began dusting the furniture and wiping everything with a damp cloth to try and get the dust off and onto the floor so we could sweep it outdoors. After we were able to get as much dust swept from the house, we began carrying buckets of water inside to wash the polished concrete floors. The cleaning took several hours, and we had not even washed our clothes or bed linens which were covered in dust. We changed the bed linens and hung the mattresses on the roof to beat them with a pole and try to get the dust out before we must sleep on them again that night. It was hard work to finish cleaning the house, and we felt and breathed dust for several days after the storm.

I had never experienced a storm like that one in my entire life. We never saw this type of thing in Missouri or Illinois. Babur said they happened every year about this time, before the monsoon season broke and the rain stopped the dust. I then began to hope that the monsoon season would start soon.

CHAPTER 9: RAMADAN IN LAHORE

The monsoon season lasted for almost forty-five days, through the last part of July, all of August, and ended by early September in Lahore. Rain would fall heavily every day in the late afternoon. Big storm clouds would appear on the horizon starting at two in the afternoon and we would be soaked by four o'clock. We always had to remember to remove the clothes that were drying on the roof of the house before the rain started. Usually the rain had stopped by early evening and we would be able to walk on the roof. The water made the rivers swell and the old walled city stank with sewage. We avoided visiting Salim during those months and family members came to our house instead because it smelled better and usually had a good breeze blowing. The temperature before and during the monsoon season was hot, about 95 degrees, and the rains just caused the weather to be humid, too. It became almost impossible to sleep in the bedrooms, so Babur and Mahji moved up to the roof at night. Ali and I had a small balcony off our bedroom where we took char pis and slept out every night. The mosquitoes were terrible and carried malaria, so we each covered ourselves with a bed sheet only allowing a part of our eyes and nose to show. Ali had purchased quinine at the drug store and we all took it every day to try to escape catching malaria from the flying clouds of mosquitoes. We had no mosquito repellant and could not purchase it in the stores around Lahore, so we took our chances every evening.   Usually by 11:00 o'clock the air turned cooler and everyone was able to sleep fitfully through the rest of the night. I occasionally woke in the night and listened to the sounds around me. You could hear some neighborhood noise, dogs barking and sometimes chickens or roosters in the night.

Early in the morning, about 5:30 a.m., the haunting calls of the Muezzin from their minarets drifted through the air. They would call the faithful to the first prayer of the day in Lahore and Mahji was always up early kneeling and performing the proper bows on her red prayer rug. I would lie on my char pi on the balcony, half asleep, totally wrapped in my sheet and listening to the melodious calls: "Allah uh Akbar, Allah uh Akbar" (God is Great) which would sound four times at the beginning of the invitation to prayer. It was a pleasant way to wake up because the calls to prayer were soft and musical. I often thought how beautiful they sounded in the mornings with no other morning road sounds to interrupt their music.   There was no place in Lahore that you could escape the five calls to prayer every day. The times for Muslim prayer are dawn, again at noon, in the middle of the afternoon, at dusk, and before bed time.

In late September the holy month of Ramadan was beginning. Ramadan is a special month of the year for over one billion Muslim throughout the world.   Ramadan, the ninth month of the Islamic calendar, is set by a combination of physical sightings of the moon and astronomical calculations.   Observance of this important month is one of the five pillars of Islam demanded by Muhammad over 1300 years ago. During Ramadan, fasting becomes obligatory for observant Muslims. Only sick people, travelers, and pregnant women are exempted from the fast. It is not just food that is abstained from during Ramadan, but drink, smoking, and marital sex. Mahji told us that anything that is pleasurable should be put off until after the month is over. One day during this holy month, Mahji received a letter from her beloved daughter Shafia in England and refused to have Ali read the letter to her until the month of Ramadan was over.

The usual schedule for this month is to have a pre-fast meal before dawn and then a post-fast meal after sunset. People often don't consume anything for between thirteen and fourteen hours each day. Many Muslims break their fast at sunset with dates, as the Prophet Muhammad was said to have done. Often friends would ask us over to their home during Ramadan to break the fast with a special meal prepared before dusk and eaten after they break their fast. During Ramadan some people would stay home on various days to read the Qur'an and contemplate its meaning. Usually, however, people went to work as always and carefully observed the fasting requirements at their jobs.

One day during the month I was out on our small balcony reading a book in the sun. The balcony overlooked the courtyard of the family that lived down stairs in the house. I believe this family owned the entire house because Ali paid rent to the father of the family once per month. I never really met the family members, but occasionally nodded as I would see one of the daughters entering or leaving their home.

Our landlord's family consisted of a father, mother, and two teen aged daughters. The courtyard below us was where they sat and did a variety of tasks such as washing clothes or relaxing during the day.

When I got up from reading my book and walked over to the edge of the high wall surrounding our balcony, I heard laughter and talk down below and quietly peeked over the wall to see into their court yard. I felt like I was invading their privacy, but wanted to find out what they were doing. I saw the mother and daughters of the house eating snacks of nuts and fruit and obviously not observing a fast of any kind. I knew they were Muslims and that during this time were supposed to be fasting, but I guessed they were not as observant as Mahji. I would often try to fast during the day so that I did not offend Mahji. I don't think she expected me to really fast, but she never ate a bite in the day light hours of Ramadan. I would occasionally sneak food so that I did not grow faint because I was not used to fasting. Ali was usually at the university and left me alone with her all day. I could not venture out alone without a male escort and grew bored and lonely during these days. During Ramadan I could not play the tape recorder during the day and so the music was stopped because I might enjoy it too much to be a good observant Muslim.

At the end of Ramadan was an important religious festival called Eid Al-Fitr. It is a celebration and rejoicing because it brings the observance of Ramadan to a close. Everyone who could afford it would sacrifice a goat or sheep during this time and the resulting feasts would be delicious.

It was considered charitable to spread the meat of your animal sacrifice around to your friends so they could have a delicious dinner, also.

Right before Eid Al-Fitr we drove through an open market place near the old city where herds of sheep and goats were being blessed and sold for slaughter. Many households slaughtered their own animals and often purchased the whole sheep on-the-hoof to take home with them. Some would purchase the animal many days ahead of the festival so they could take it home and feed it extra food in their back yards to fatten it up before slaughter. Ali did not want to have to slaughter an animal personally, so both Ali and Salim purchased a goat together and it stayed somewhere on Salim's roof until its day of doom. The children fed it to fatten it up before its sacrifice. When it was slaughtered by a local religious butcher, the two brothers split the goat in half and we received lots of meat and two of the hoofs. The goat meat went into our refrigerator and on the festival day Mahji prepared the most delicious goat meat mixed with rice, raisins, spices, and curry that I have ever eaten in my life. I could not get enough of the special dish and kept asking for more during the festival's banquet.

During the festival we went to the old walled city to have tea with Salim, and Mahji, in a loud voice, demanded that we should give some of his goat meat to a poor widow who lived close by. I asked to go along on the visit when I found out what was happening, so Mahji, Fozia, and I took a small amount of goat meat wrapped in several green leaves of a tree and walked approximately two alley ways down from Salim's to the home of the widow. When we arrived, I could not believe that what I was standing in front of was someone's home. Opening directly onto the alley and two feet away from the sewer, was a very small door leading to a one room hovel. There was only a blanket over the doorway and as Mahji called her friends name we entered her home saying "Salaam Al Akum" as a greeting.

The woman was over 60 years old, dressed in a tattered navy blue burkah, and she lived in a house with no furniture except a char pi. The room in the house was about ten feet wide by ten feet long and had only one door. There was no bathroom or running water in the house, except the sewer outside the door. I was shocked by the condition in which this woman lived. She was a very poor widow whose husband had died at least twenty years ago. She had no children and no one to take care of her during her old age. Mahji was one of her only friends and any time she was in the old walled city she visited the widow's house, always bringing her little presents. The widow had a fire burning in the middle of the floor and her only fuel was the dung paddies she had collected herself from the street and dried.

Mahji gave her the meat surrounded tightly in leaves and wished her a good holiday. I tried to smile at her as I was looking around her small room. The widow was overcome with gratitude for the gift from Mahji and kissed her hand while Mahji mumbled something to her in Urdu under her breath, I believe a prayer, and fought to pull her hand back. The widow stripped off the leaves, took out the chunk of goat meat and, cutting it up in smaller pieces, she popped it into a kettle of water cooking on the stove. She would probably eat that food for several days and be grateful for the gift from her friend. She offered us chai tea while we at her home, but Mahji made excuses so that we could leave almost immediately. It was obvious to me that Mahji did not want to take the widow's only bit of tea and drink it. We left the house after only a few minutes and returned to Salim's home.

I am sure that Mahji's frequent gifts of food and old clothing kept this poor widow alive. Only because Mahji had several sons who looked after her life and health could she live any differently than this widow lived. There is no Social Security or Medicare in Pakistan, and widows and orphans have an extremely rough time trying to make a living.

I was strolling on our roof looking at the view one afternoon and was able to watch as a neighbor slaughtered his own goat. He had hung the poor animal from a hook on a tree with a rope and then after several prayers he grabbed the goat's small horns and cut its throat with a sharp knife. I heard the goat bleating loudly and then, very suddenly, it stopped as the knife traced a red line across its throat. Goat blood dripped in a stream down to the dirt below the tree. He let it bleed to death slowly while hanging upside down and then after about one hour cut it down and started dividing up the meat between relatives who had come over to watch the slaughter. He worked quickly on the dirt ground, cutting and wrapping the meat in leaves from the death tree. Each relative was thankful for the gift of meat and left quickly to get it home to cook.

Several days later Mahji cooked a soup containing our goat's ankles and hooves. Nothing on the sacrificed animal was thrown away. I am glad I did not see any regional dishes with the goat's head involved in the recipe.   Ali assured me this soup was a delicacy and I watched as the sticky bubbling brew boiled in a large pot. She mixed onions and other spices with the goat parts and simmered it over a low flame most of the day. The smell of cooking goat's feet wafted through the air of our apartment all day long. That evening at dinner we all tasted the soup. It was actually rather good, but if you let any of it dry on your hand or the table the mixture became as sticky as glue.   I referred to this soup later as "glue soup" and Ali translated my words to Mahji which caused her to laugh for several minutes.   I guess the soup was full of protein and many people in Lahore ate "glue soup" using goat's hooves for the rich ingredients.   It was considered a regional favorite.

In October, Ali came home one day and announced to me that it was possible for me to get my Bachelor of Arts degree from Punjab University. He described the process which included some heavy studying and a day of testing in a local women's college. If I wanted to do this studying I could return to the United States with a Bachelor's degree from Pakistan.   The university system in Pakistan is patterned after British schools and a student can study, take written tests in English, and obtain their degree if they receive high enough marks in the tests. This was known as being an "external student" and Ali would register me so I could take the tests.

My boredom during the day was beginning to be overwhelming to me so the prospect of accomplishing something educational instead of just hanging around the house was exciting. I practically begged Ali to find the correct books on the test subjects so I could begin studying for it. Ali said that I had to choose from several subjects that were available to me for a major. I decided upon Indo-Pakistani History and English Literature as my majors.

Within three days Ali had the books at our house and I started my studies to pass the university tests. I began reading all of them and outlining important segments of Pakistani Muslim history that I would be required to write about in an essay. Days passed and I was engrossed in my work toward getting this degree. I set up a desk in the small room on the stairs leading to the roof. Here noise from the house or Mahji cleaning and cooking would not bother me. My only company in my makeshift office was a couple of small gecko lizards that stayed on the wall near the ceiling and looked at me. They were good companions and I must admit I spent time watching them also. My make-shift office was small, about eight feet long and maybe six feet wide, but I moved a char pi up to the room and had Ali buy me a cheap table and chair. The light for reading came from a large window looking out on to the street in front of the house. I did not have a lamp and really didn't need one because most days were filled with sunshine and I would not be reading after sunset.

Days passed and I was engrossed in my work toward a degree. I had married Ali and left Southern Illinois University after only one and a half years of school, so I did not have a Bachelor's degree. Even though I suspected that a Bachelor's degree from Punjab University would not be equal to a degree from SIU, it was better to go home to the United States with something concrete, so I dedicated myself to my studies.

The two major subjects were very interesting and I enjoyed learning about history of the country. However, I also had to read additional books such as European history and basic science. These subjects did not interest me as much and I had to buckle down and force myself to work hard to get through them.

I learned a lot about the centuries of Moghul Emperors and the story of Muslims in India, the British Raj and the break-up of the Indian empire culminating in the partition of India. The partition created East and West Pakistan and is still causing armed strife in the region. I have heard that some of India wishes that the 1947 partition never took place and that the Indian continent was still intact. They believe it was the final curse of the British Raj to separate India into countries that fight each other now. Of course, most of the books were written by Pakistani writers and reflected the Muslim viewpoint rather than giving the broader story, but I did not care. I was working toward the only degree I could get during these years. I would worry about additional education later in my life. In English literature I studied writers such as Dickens, Shakespeare, and more. I read "David Copperfield" and some short stories that would be included in the questions on the tests. Every spare minute was used for reading the materials I would ultimately be tested on for my degree.

One day Ali brought home one of his friends from the University. Mohammed Zaheer was an economics professor who had been with Ali in Indiana before he moved to Carbondale. Zaheer had received his Ph. D. in economics and was a very intelligent person. He was about thirty-eight years old, married, and had three handsome sons. Dr. Zaheer spoke perfect English and I enjoyed chatting with him. He wanted to invite us to his home for dinner in about one week and was visiting to ask me what types of food I liked to eat. I thought that was extremely thoughtful because many times when I would go to other homes I was unable to eat the food because of the extreme spices cooked into the meals. The Zaheer family lived near the university campus and had a comfortable three bedroom bungalow.

One week later we drove over to their home for the dinner party. Mrs. Zaheer was busy cooking in the kitchen when we arrived so Zaheer took me to meet her there. She was a delightful, happy woman who smiled and laughed constantly. She had long black hair in a braid down her back, but a few strands of fuzzy curls popped out around her face. Her entire face lit up when she was smiling, which was often. She was wearing a simple chemise and pajamas in a tan silk fabric. Her scarf was tied behind her neck to keep it out of the food that was being prepared.

Her name was Nina, and she was Zaheer's second cousin. She spoke little English, but we immediately liked each other and I sensed she was intelligent. She did not care if Ali saw her face and neither did Zaheer. They were Muslim, but not so strict that they believed women should hide in the back bedroom when other men were in the house. They had three handsome young boys whose ages ranged from three years old, close to eight years, and the oldest around ten years. Two of the boys spoke English because their father had been teaching them since they were very young. Only the youngest could not speak English, but was using Urdu in short sentences. He was small and shy of the blonde American woman and would run from me into his mother's arms if I approached and tried to pick him up.

During dinner I asked Zaheer to tell me how he met his wife and married her. He told me that he has seen her once as a young girl at family gatherings. Zaheer was about ten years older than Nina and asked his father to talk to her parents about marriage as he grew older. When she was sixteen and Zaheer was around twenty-six years old they were formally engaged. A marriage took place one year later; they had only met twice during their engagement, in a room full of other relatives as chaperones. He knew he loved her immediately and apparently she loved him, too. It was one of those rare matches that sometimes worked out. Both husband and wife were happy and cared much about their partner in life, even though they had only met three brief times before they were married.

The meal went well and Nina's cooking was delicious. After several hours we said goodbye and returned to our apartment.

Zaheer was an open and truthful person, and one time when he had dropped by to pick up Ali he asked me some questions. Ali was out of the room at the time getting ready to go with Zaheer to the university for a meeting. We were having tea at the kitchen table and he asked me about the story Ali told everyone concerning my father being a Swedish diplomat. I could not bring myself to lie to Zaheer and told him all about our American wedding, my father and mother's occupations, and how Ali and I met right before he was forced to leave the country because of his visa problem. I spoke in a subdued tone of voice so that Ali did not hear me and implored Zaheer never to tell that I had revealed this information to him. He promised he would not tell anyone, and then he asked one more important question. Had Ali finished his Ph.D. in Carbondale? I immediately said that he had finished everything except his doctorial thesis, which he was working on when we got married. Zaheer was shocked about this revelation and, shaking his head, informed me that Ali has assured everyone at the university he had completed his Ph.D. – but never produced any real proof – saying it was somehow caught up in red tape in America.

I somehow felt better having revealed the truth to someone in Pakistan, but I prayed Ali would never find out about my betrayal of his lies to his friend and colleague.

Zaheer had sensed that Ali was lying to everyone and he wanted to know the truth. He promised to keep my secret and I believed him. Neither of us understood the reasons for the deceptions or why it was so important to Ali to appear to be something he was not.

During the weeks of study that I was trying to concentrate on every day, an interesting thing happened: our toilets blocked up. The sewage system was a simple one but somehow there was a clog in it now. The landlord would not take care of anything in the house, so Ali was forced to find someone to fix the toilets and find them fast.

During this time Mahji was visiting Salim's house and we were alone for days at our apartment. We had been going out to dinner at several restaurants while Mahji was gone, and I had enjoyed the solitude very much. Somehow, Ali was able to find plumbers who would visit the house at approximately 11:00 in the morning, so he made sure he came home to the apartment to talk to them about the plumbing. I am not sure if he realized who they were when he employed them, but when he greeted them at the bottom of the stairs he found out that the plumbers were Pathans. Pathans are a group of semi-nomadic people who are originally from the frontier region between Pakistan and Afghanistan. Pathans are Muslims and speak "Pashto", a language that is similar to Punjabi, but not exactly the same.

The Pathans are noted as fierce fighters, and throughout history they have offered strong resistance to invaders. Throughout history no country or fighting force has been able to win a war with the Pathans. Even Alexander the

Great needed to bargain with the tribal groups from this region. The British attempted to subdue the Pathans in a series of expeditions in the late 19th century, but were finally forced to offer them a semi-autonomous area called the North-West Frontier Province, between the border of British India and that of Afghanistan. When Pakistan was formed it annexed the Pathan border regions, but never subdued the war-like Pathans. The Russians also tried to subdue the Pathans in Afghanistan and, of course, were unable to complete their goals there, also.

These are the fierce people that make up the Taliban movement of Afghanistan and they had many sympathizers in northern Pakistan. I had heard stories of Pathan rifles being heavily decorated in silver and that Pathan men were always armed and extremely dangerous. One of the reasons we never traveled as far north as the Khyber Pass was because of the danger of running into a band of Pathan warriors.

Ali rushed up the steps and found me in the kitchen. He immediately dragged me to the back bedroom and told me to stay in there and keep the door bolted until the men were gone. I glanced over his shoulder as the men were starting to come up the steps and they hesitated on the porch outside the door. I could see a group of three very tall men garbed in white robes, even covering their heads. They looked like three wraiths standing with wooden walking sticks in their hands on the porch. I sensed an immediate danger and so I slammed the bedroom door shut and moved the bolt in place to lock it. Ali invited the three men into the living room and they all began talking in a language I did not understand. They talked for fifteen minutes and Ali explained the trouble with the plumbing. I suppose they were determining a price for the work, also.

After what seemed like a long while, the men left the living room and walked back down the stairs to look over the bathroom and plumbing system. At that time Ali came to my door and asked me to unlock it for a moment. He proceeded to tell me in a hushed voice that Pathans were famous for abducting woman and holding them for ransom. The captives would be taken to the Northwest Frontier Region and no one could follow the Pathans, it was too dangerous. I must stay behind the locked door until after the men had finished the job and were gone. If they saw a blonde woman in this house, they might target us for a future kidnapping, and that would not be very healthy for anyone involved.

I quickly locked the door again and Ali went to supervise the Pathans work in the bathroom. I heard muffled hammering and loud talking in a language I did not recognize for a while. I stayed in the bedroom with the door bolted and tried to read my books, but was nervous that something ominous might happen. After about two hours the Pathan men left and Ali came and told me everything was all right and I could leave the bedroom again. I was relieved the plumbing was fixed and the men had left the house. I don't believe the Pathans ever saw me, so we all thought we would not have any trouble in the future from these rough, war-like people.

Even though Osama Bin Laden was born and raised in Saudi Arabia, his rhetoric appeals to the ultra conservative Pathan warriors who live in the regions of Afghanistan and the Northwest Frontier Province of Pakistan. These fierce Muslim warriors, who appear to be lifted right out of the Middle Ages, are sheltering his band of Al Quida terrorists and will continue to do so until every last one of them is killed in battles with American soldiers. When Pathans are finally gone from their ancestral homes and territories a proud part of historical India goes with them to their graves, and I cannot help myself from examining their culture and bravery with an admiration for their untamed nature. However, their rough treatment of woman and girls, their adherence to extremism in religion and their inability to change into a modern community will ultimately cause their extermination. It is just a matter of time until their culture becomes extinct on this planet.

That evening we went out to my favorite restaurant, a Tanduri chicken place that was famous in Lahore. Ali knew the owner, who was a tall robust Punjabi man with a huge handlebar mustache, so when we walked in the door the waiters immediately rushed over to seat us at our table and take our order. I ordered chai tea and one of the chicken dishes with rice and an extra order of plain yogurt. The restaurant was filled with small tables and rough wooden chairs in a large open room. The only people I saw seated at the tables seemed to be men. Very few women or couples generally went out to dinner together in Lahore unless it was at the large western hotels. We were seated at a table near a wall and away from other men eating dinner. A few of these men turned and looked at us as we walked to our table. There were no votive candles or bright decorations to make the ambiance of the place inviting to anyone. Ali informed me that everyone knew about the wonderful chicken served in this restaurant and that take-out food was a big part of the owner's business.

It was delicious, and both Ali and I enjoyed the Tanduri chicken. The owner came to our table and talked in Urdu to Ali for a few minutes. He seemed jolly and friendly to Ali and very polite to me. He only knew a few words in English but he was able to understand my personal thanks for the delicious meal. He did not allow us to pay for dinner and argued for about ten minutes with Ali as we left that evening. I heard later that the restaurant owner was a childhood friend of Ali's and had been born in the old walled city near Ali's home. It was an interesting day which ended with an excellent meal. Mahji was returning to our apartment tomorrow and would resume her cooking duties in the kitchen. I don't believe that Mahji had ever gone to a restaurant in her entire life and, if asked, would not consent to do so.

CHAPTER 10: TAXILA AND BEYOND

In October 1969, we were planning a road trip to northern Pakistan including the capital of Islamabad, Ralwalpindi, and a few villages in the Swat Valley. The trip from Islamabad to Swat Valley takes about eight or nine hours over mountain roads. There was a village in Swat called Gilgit which has numerous picturesque sites and a famous bazaar for shopping. It is considered to be the Switzerland of Pakistan and located on the ancient trading route nomadic tribes used to travel between China and Pakistan through the Hindu Kush. This entire trip would last about five or six days and would take us through the famous archeological site of Taxila near Rawalpindi and Islamabad.

Ali and I wanted to have another person with us in the car for added security and he asked his friend, Shahji, if he could take off the time from his work. Luckily, he had saved vacation time and was able to use a few days to accompany us for what proved to be a very interesting tour of historic places in northern Pakistan. Excitement was high for the three of us as we started out on our road trip by heading toward Gujranwala, Sialkot, and Islamabad in our gray Volkswagen Beetle automobile. I sat in the front passenger seat, Ali drove, and the back seat was occupied by Shahji with some food in a rustic cooler for the trip. Our luggage was in the trunk and tied on the roof. We had also brought along several jackets, hats, wool gloves, and scarves for possible cold weather. We would be able to buy needed supplies on our travels and planned to eat at some of the local hotels.

Shahji was not from a wealthy family so Ali offered to pay his way in order to have the additional person as a companion and guide. Shahji had been on this route many years earlier and could help with the driving and navigation duties. We arrived in Islamabad in the middle of the afternoon on the first day and decided to tour the city before picking a hotel. Shahji had a distant cousin who owned a rug store in town so we headed there as our first stop. The store was not large, but was piled high to the ceiling with folded and rolled Afgan wool rugs of every size and color.

We parked the car in front of the shop and walked inside. I entered the narrow door and walked on the old wooden plank floor with Shahji and Ali heading toward the back of the store, my eyes swept over the wool rugs hanging from the walls in display. The wide variety of colors were mainly reds, rusts, browns, yellows, oranges, blues, and tans making each rug a tapestry of wool pile. I ran my hands lightly along the width of each rug as I slowly walked and marveled at the quality of the weaving. Turning to Ali, I inquired about the price and if we could afford to purchase a few to send back to the States. He said he would ask, but doubted we had the money for such an extravagance as rugs.

The men at the back of the store got up from their seats at a small table and walked toward us with broad smiles on their faces. They were all dressed in traditional garb, long white cotton shirts and baggy pants made of a medium weight fabric. I believe at first they thought they had some customers and then Shahji was recognized by his cousin and the men started talking very fast in Punjabi and hugging each other. I was introduced as Ali's American wife and the men shyly stared at me for a few minutes. Of course, my clothes were appropriate because I was wearing the pajama pants and chemise with a shawl over my shoulders. I had gotten used to these traditional Pakistani clothes and even enjoyed the comfort they provided me. None of my casual daytime clothes were cut in a tight form fitting style like the fancy party outfits that I had tailored for festive occasions such as weddings.

So these men and anyone else I met during this journey to the north could not evaluate my young body or have any reason to believe I was an American girl with no morals. I was displaying all of the modesty of a local Muslim girl and kept my body covered from head to toe, but without wearing a burkah or traditional veil. I refused to cover my face and most of the time my hair was uncovered unless I was instructed by someone to quickly cover my head because of religious reasons or the person whom I was meeting was offended by my easy style. It was difficult for me to get used to the scarf or shawl around my shoulders and sometimes it would fall from my shoulders or get caught in the crook of my elbows. The rest of my clothing was comfortable and easy to wear and move about in on our road trip.

The cousins immediately offered Chai tea and cookies and we ate and drank while the men talked in the back of the store. I was given the freedom to look over the many rugs stockpiled around the walls of the shop.   It was heavenly, and I loved touching the wool and found myself smiling at the colors while inhaling their musty cloth.   I envied these men and their rug store. I wanted to own this stockpile of wool and sit, sleep, eat, and play on them all in my own home. But Ali told me we could only afford the price of one small prayer rug to take home with us. This decision was disappointing, but I was allowed to pick out a wool prayer rug a little larger than a door mat in America. The men rolled it up, tied it with a cord, and gave it to Ali for safe keeping after he paid about twenty-five dollars for it. We were also invited to dinner at their home later in the evening so their wives could meet the American girl while Shahji talked to his cousins. We accepted their invitation and told them we would return later for dinner, but now we would find a hotel to check into for the night.

It was about 2:00 o'clock in the afternoon when we finally left the rug store to find lodgings for the evening. There were plenty of small Guest Hostels or British style hotels with real beds and bathrooms. We found a small place where we could get two rooms adjacent to each other and purchased them for the evening. Ali paid for Shahji's room, gave him his key, and we got the key to our own room. We were afraid to leave any of our suitcases or belongings in the rooms while we were away so we did not unpack the car at this time. Instead we decided to go to the bazaar before we went to dinner at Shahji's cousin's home.

Driving down many small streets, Shahji directed us toward the major bazaar in the middle of down town. The bazaar had small stores with wool shawls, blankets, and animal skin hats and coats, mostly made in Kashmir or Kabul and brought over the border in caravans. The wool was finely woven and soft to the touch, with embroidery in many colors. I enjoyed looking at everything and tried on some of the lamb skin hats, but did not buy anything.

Walking through the shopping district in Islamabad was different than in Lahore's many bazaars. Because of the cities proximity to the Northern Territories there were Afghan men and women walking around the area doing their own shopping. The Afghan women were heavily veiled in black burkahs with only mesh eye coverings as their windows to the world. They followed their men several paces behind with their heads down, watching their feet, and only looking toward the backs of their husbands, brothers, or fathers.

The men dressed in long robes and lamb skin head coverings that made them look very much like something out of the Bible. They often carried long rifles that resembled guns made in the American civil war era. All of them had rows of bullets on heavy leather bandoliers over their shoulders. The rifles had inlaid ivory and silver on their wooden stocks and were quite long. The men always had heavy dark beards covering their faces. They looked like savage fighters and I could easily imagine how they held off the British army throughout the 1890's and were never subdued by their larger forces. These tribal people were definitely fierce warriors.

Ali made sure that my head was well covered in a black shawl that I carried with me. It was cool weather and I did not mind being covered and even occasionally held the shawl edge over my mouth. I also made sure that I never looked directly at anyone, especially men, or smiled at them. I did not want to ask for any trouble in this rough town. Ali and Shahji stayed close to me as we walked through the bazaar. The last British battles with the Afghan tribesmen occurred in 1935, and I was seeing these tribal men just thirty-five years later. Nothing had changed in the thirty-five years and it almost seemed as if I was watching an old movie from that era. We were safe in this populated bazaar, but we did not want to call attention to ourselves in case someone chose to follow us to the lonely roads going into the Swat Valley and mountain passes.

It was time for us to visit the home of Shahji's cousins for dinner so we left the bazaar and drove to the residential areas of the city. The house we finally located was a large white concrete square home with flat roof and high wall surrounding the yard and building. The gate into the driveway was opened by a servant and we drove the Volkswagen into the walled area. We were escorted into the house by the servant and greeted by the men of the family who were seated in the large living room on sofas covered in plastic.

I murmured the Muslim greeting and then was shown into the kitchen by Shahji's cousin, where the women of the family were preparing the meal. The kitchen was a large room with several windows. Iron pots and copper pans with lids were boiling on various gas burners sitting on the concrete floor. Aromas from the spices for the curry and lamb dishes were strong in this room. All spices were in small dishes or glass jars so that the several female cooks could get at them easily while shaking the bottle or spooning some into each dish. Different colors and food consistency in the pots told me what was cooking and I immediately recognized rice, curried chicken, and curried lamb with spinach. I was introduced to the three women and I automatically repeated the proper greetings. The women laughed and greeted me in a very friendly manner. One pulled over a simple wooden chair for me and motioned toward me to sit and relax while I watched them cook. I was offered Chai tea which I immediately accepted and drank while they were finishing the cooking. All the men were gathered in the living room talking while they waited for dinner to be ready.

Soon dinner was served. A young boy about eight years old put the cooked food on the dining table located near the living room while the women kept some food in the kitchen for themselves. None of the women would show themselves in the dining room because Ali was there and he was not a family member. I walked into the dining room and sat down with the men at the table. I had made up my mind many months ago that I would not let the "purdah" customs about separation of women and men keep me hidden in the back rooms.

Some of the men knew English and we had a pleasant meal with discussions about America and what I had seen so far visiting Pakistan. I could not eat much of the prepared food because it had too much spice and peppers mixed with each dish. But the rice dish with lentils was mild and very good with plain yogurt placed on top. I tasted all of the food dishes, but only out of politeness. One of the women boiled two eggs for me to eat with the rice. After dinner we had tea in the living room while sitting on the several sofas with plastic coverings. The floors were covered with beautiful wool Afghan rugs.

At approximately 9:00 o'clock we said our goodbyes and left the house to drive back to the hotel. We had to leave for Ralwalpindi and on to Taxila the next day, so needed to get some sleep. At the hotel we unloaded everything from the car into our hotel room. We did not want anyone breaking into the car in the middle of the night to steal our clothes or meager possessions. The hotel room was small with twin beds, a chair, and small table. A lamp was placed on the table. The room had a small bathroom with shower. No towels, soap, or toilet paper was available in this hotel. But we had brought our own personal supplies with us because we knew it would be difficult to find it in the cheap hotels we were going to be using. We did not have the money for the expensive hotels that most foreign travelers visited when in the country. I would have enjoyed staying in the more luxurious hotels in the big cities, but knew how much they cost; for the three of us to stay in them would have been expensive.

The next morning we loaded up the car with our belongings and headed toward the archeological site of Taxila, about 30 miles down the Grand Trunk Road. Taxila is a very ancient and interesting town in eastern Punjab which was founded in the seventh or sixth century BCE according to local legend. One of the oldest known Hindu shrines is located in Taxila. The area had been occupied by the Persians and the Macedonian conqueror, Alexander the Great, in 326 BC. At the time Alexander arrived there, Taxilan territory extended modestly from the Indus River to the Jhelum River. Alexander's famous horse, Bucephalus, died at 30 years of age near Taxila and Alexander built a large memorial to him there.

We used most of the morning looking around the Taxila ruins and viewed the museum which held many pieces of gold jewelry, beads, coins, pottery, and other items from the archeological digs. As we were leaving the area we encountered some local villagers and I was amazed to find that two young girls had blonde hair and green eyes. I was told that Alexander and his army left much more in the area than just golden Greek coins. Many more of the local citizens show the genetic make-up of Greek and Macedonian warriors with their light complexion, blonde or light brown hair and eye color. The blond girls are considered very beautiful all over Pakistan and many were thought to be good marriage material because of their fair complexions.

From this interesting archeological site we traveled about one hundred miles toward Peshawar which was several hours away and to the north. Peshawar is an important city on the border between Pakistan and Afghanistan. The interesting highlight here is the Old City – a brawl of vendors selling everything from tribal jewelry to leather pistol holsters. Clopping horse-drawn Tongas (two-wheeled horse-drawn rickshaws) choke the streets, and fearsome-looking Pashtuns, Afghans, and Chitrali citizens are everywhere. I wanted to travel over the Khyber Pass into Kabul, but Ali and Shahji said the trip was too dangerous because of bandits.

A short distance outside of Peshawar is the Smugglers' Bazaar. We decided to walk through and look around the Smugglers' Bazaar to see if there was anything we might wish to buy. We pulled over the Volkswagen and parked it in a bare piece of ground where we could leave the car but still observe it from a distance. It was a short walk to rows of brightly colored tents with stacks of cloth, boxes, and pots in front of each tent. The people were different than any I had ever seen before in Pakistan. The women were wearing very brightly colored striped blouses and skirts with very small black hats. They did not attempt to cover their faces or arms, and were rapidly dancing to musical instruments resembling small guitars. The men played music with drums and string instruments and the women danced with their colorful skirts whirling and their long black braids swinging around their heads. Small girls and boys would follow us around begging for coins while we walked among the tents looking at objects for sale.

I picked up some shoe boxes and noticed that inside all of them was the inscription "Made in China". In 1968 America did not have trading relations with China and to see this label was rather interesting to me. When I showed the box to Ali he told me that the gypsies in this camp traveled by horseback, over the mountains to trade in China. The horses were small but strong and could live in the high mountain terrain and thin air. Gypsies brought back to Pakistan many items that they sold in bazaars and camps such as the one we were visiting. What we were viewing in the camp were the smuggled merchandise from China, which was the basis for this interesting economy and the only livelihood of these gypsies. Ali would not let me buy anything at the bazaar because he said they were charging me three times the amount they would have charged a Pakistani, simply because I was American. We left after looking around for about one hour and went back to Peshawar to find a hotel for the night.

The next morning before we left Peshawar to head higher into the mountains we went to the Old City bazaar and walked around for about one hour. As we were passing several shopping areas which were in a block of small, old, wooden, one room buildings, Ali stopped at one and took me inside. The small building had wooden boxes piled up against the wall, some open and displaying their contents. Located in each of the boxes were dried plants and herbs. Ali explained that this shop sold opium, hashish, marijuana, and other drugs that had been brought into Peshawar from Afghanistan. I stared in surprise because I had never seen any of these drugs and only read how addicting they were to any person who used them. The shop keeper in the corner was sitting on a barrel and smoking a pipe. He and Ali exchanged a few Punjabi words and then Ali told me it was time to leave.

We hurried out of the building while I inquired if these drugs were legal in Pakistan. Ali said that they were only sold in Peshawar and if we were caught with any in our car in Lahore we might be arrested. It did not matter; I was not considering purchasing any illegal drugs anyway. In Carbondale, Illinois I had never tried any of these drugs and had been too sheltered in my life to even know how to use them. It was interesting to see how they were sold, usually to local citizens, and what these drugs cost. Ali said they were very cheap, and anyone who wanted them could purchase handfuls of drugs without being arrested in Peshawar.

We began our mountain driving by heading on a single lane highway toward the district of Swat. This was a high mountain region in northern Pakistan which was supposed to be comparable to Switzerland. It turned out to have the loveliest scenery, with lush meadows, hot springs, and views of several colossal mountain peaks. But to get there we had to drive many hours on winding mountain highways. I became extremely car sick and had no drugs such as Dramamine or any other method to stop the nausea. Most of the highway trip I was curled up in the back seat of the

Volkswagen with a paper bag near me so that I didn't mess up the car. A few times we had to stop so that I could get out of the car and move to the side of the road to throw up. I was not feeling very well all during this mountain trip. Ali drove with Shahji sitting in the front passenger seat, navigating.

I was very happy when we finally arrived in Gilgit, a small town situated in the middle of a large green mountain valley. The weather was cold and we needed our coats and heavy clothes. The valley was beautiful with terraced slopes where farmers planted crops and boys herded the long haired sheep. Women here did not cover their faces, but would not look you straight in the eyes because of modesty. However, the woman could be smiling often and seemed happy. In these northern towns people wore wool clothes and heavy wool hats with rolled edges. Some of the men would be wearing fur coats and many had fur hats, but usually wore just a sweater over their light weight wool shirt and pants.

Two miles out of Gilgit are a pair of fifteen foot high Buddha's carved in the rock face of a mountain side. They go back to the fifth century and are ignored by the local population who are entirely devoted to Islam. At this extreme northern part of Pakistan you are very close to Kashmir, and if there had not been a declaration of war between India and Pakistan we could have traveled to this area easily. Kashmiri wool was sold in the small bazaar in Gilgit, and I could see that it was extremely fine and soft. Ali purchased a bolt of Kashmiri wool cloth for about one hundred dollars. His intention was to take the wool back to Lahore and have a suit made by a tailor. Shahji found a wool hat to buy, and I tried on several fur hats made of lamb's skin. I finally settled on an ivory and carved wooden jewelry box that I found in a small shop. It was beautifully carved with inlaid pieces of ivory and about ten inches square. It cost approximately $15.00 and I was happy to have it at that price.

We stayed the evening in a wonderful hotel on the side of a mountain. There were fireplaces in every room and no central heating. It felt like we were staying in a chalet in the mountains of Switzerland. We sat on balconies outside our rooms and watched as the sun slowly slid behind the mountains. That night we could see the aurora borealis or northern lights from our balcony. I had never seen them before and considered it an extraordinary sight.

The next morning we continued shopping for a while before heading back toward Peshawar and finally Lahore. It took us two and a half days of driving to get back, but we needed to hurry because both Ali and Shahji had to return to work. The trip back was just a whirl of driving over mountainous roads and car sickness for me laying in the backseat. When we finally arrived in Peshawar I was happy to switch seats with Shahji and finally begin watching the scenery again.

We arrived in Lahore and drove Shahji to his home before we returned to our second floor apartment. Our trip was over but would live in my memory for many years afterward. I felt like I had traveled to the ends of the earth and back again. I began to believe that people were the same everywhere in the world except for language and tradition. The historical sites we visited on this trip were by far the most interesting I had ever imagined in my young life.

CHAPTER 11: THE UNIVERSITY OF THE PUNJAB

Ali had been teaching at the University of the Punjab since before my arrival in Lahore. The University had several campuses and Ali taught at the newer campus near the edge of the city. The historical main campus was located near the old walled city of Lahore and had been founded by the British colonial authorities in 1882. The new campus was located about 10 minutes from our apartment and was built in the middle of 1,700 acres of lush green fields. An irrigation canal flowed nearby the campus and in addition to classrooms and tall buildings there was a nice, but simple, medical clinic for the students and faculty.

I had visited Ali's classroom occasionally, and there were some university social events involving the professors and their wives that I could attend and get to know a few people. Almost everyone spoke excellent English, except a few of the wives, but people were very friendly at these parties, so I had little difficulty communicating. The men and women at the university did not sit separately or observe Purdah and seemed to be among the more modern thinking individuals that I met in Lahore. The sophistication of people on this campus was probably due to the fact that most of the professors were educated in America or England and had returned to Pakistan after receiving advanced degrees.

Usually when a young woman student attended the new campus, but lived in the older part of Lahore, she would arrive on campus wearing a burkah, but often she ended up discarding it after a very short time. Both men and women attended the same classrooms and were offered the same courses of study. I also noticed that there were several women professors teaching in these classrooms. At the few social activities where Ali and I would visit other professors, many of the people would ask me about my life in America. I had to be careful to lie to them as Ali had instructed me to do. It was not easy for me to tell lies and I became embarrassed every time anyone asked a question about my father's occupation or if Ali had finished his Ph.D. in America. I could not tell anyone the truth about Ali and so I tried my best to avoid both subjects when his friends asked probing questions.

By late November 1969, I had been studying for six months the several subjects I would be tested on for my Bachelor of Arts degree. In Pakistan, students could study at home and take tests at several college locations depending on the specific subjects and what sex the students happen to be. Men and women were not allowed to take the final tests together, so I was assigned to a "women only" testing site. I was informed in a letter from the university that I would be expected at a local women's college in early December to take the tests. The testing was to last about four hours and therefore I needed to bring several pens with me because all of the tests were written essays.

Exam day soon arrived for my testing and Ali delivered me to the women's college site. I entered the old building and found my classroom with desks and chairs placed in straight lines the length of the room. The college was an old dilapidated building that was two stories high with many small classrooms. At a table in the front of the classroom were two women who would act as monitors for the women sitting for the tests.

I was given a student number and a printed booklet which I had to go through and answer all the questions. Everyone wrote directly on the blank newsprint paper pages of the test booklet and then turned it into the monitors at the front of the room. I sat down in a wooden chair at a small desk away from some of the other girls and began to look though the booklet slowly. These were not easy questions, but I began to slowly answer each one and hoped my memory was correct. I used simple and straightforward English words so that the individual grading the test booklet would not be confused or misunderstand my answers. I tried to be very detailed in my answers and not forget any piece of information that could give me a few extra points from the professor grading the test.

Time went by very swiftly. Almost four hours later, we were given a ten minute warning before we were to hand in our test booklets. I carefully went over all my answers to check them for accuracy and then picked up my booklet, walked to the front of the room and handed it to the room monitor. I did not know how well I had crafted my answers, or if I had succeeded in passing, but I was happy to have it over and felt that if I could pass these tests I would have something to show for my two years in Pakistan.

Ali was outside waiting for me in the Volkswagen, and as he drove me to our apartment we talked about some of my test answers. He said it would take several months before I found out my scores. Ali said he would inquire among other professors who might be doing the grading and maybe he could insure I received passing scores. He knew this made me nervous because I wanted to pass the tests based on my own efforts, but Ali assured me that many professors would not pass a student who had not offered a small bribe. I was shocked by that statement but realized that most jobs, exams, and other areas of Pakistani life were furthered by bribes and "baksheesh" offered to officials who had power. If Ali inquired enough he would be able to find the professor grading my test. If we were lucky it would be someone he knew in Lahore.

During December in Lahore there had been several large political demonstrations, led by student radicals, through the streets. I never knew exactly what everyone was protesting, but it was not safe for me to be out on the streets during these times. In retribution for these demonstrations, the government closed the universities and colleges for short periods of time to try to stop the students. One afternoon, Ali's nephew, Babur, came bursting into the apartment and told me in broken English that he had heard Moshe Dyan's son was found at a private elite college in Lahore. I just laughed at him and told him that I doubted Moshe Dyan, the distinguished Israeli general, would ever send his son anywhere near a Muslim country like Pakistan.

Babur could not understand why I didn't believe the story he was telling me. Babur had no concept of the countries outside his small world and he and his friends believed any rumor spread in hatred around the schools. Israeli General Moshe Dyan was infamous in Arab and Muslim countries because of the total defeat of Egyptian and Syrian forces during the 1967 Arab/Israeli six day war. Hatred of anything Israeli was prevalent in Pakistan and especially among the young boys who had been told that the Israelis had somehow "stolen" the victory from Egypt, Syria, and Jordan.

I did wonder if something harmful had happened to an innocent boy that might have been mistaken for Moshe Dyan's son at the college. I never found out if a real person had been beaten or killed because students believed he was Jewish. There were some Pakistani Christian families in Lahore, but I had not heard of any Jewish families living there.

One of the few professors that Ali respected was a Christian man named Dr. Feroz. This man was approximately fifty years old and married to a pretty Pakistani Christian woman named Mary. They had two young children, a ten year old boy and an eight year old girl. Christian families were often discriminated against in this Muslim country and Dr. Feroz had to work very hard to be employed as a professor in the University of the Punjab. He had an American Ph.D. degree in philosophy and was a very good humored gentleman. We visited his home near the university several times where they served us dinner or tea in the afternoons. However, Ali never invited Dr. Feroz and his family to our apartment for dinner. I believe it was because his mother would not have liked the Christian family and probably would refuse to cook for them. In Islam, Christians, Hindus, Buddhists, and Parsees are considered infidels and are treated as second class citizens.

One afternoon during a tea party at Dr. Feroz's house he told us an interesting story of an incident that had threatened his family right after his return from America. The family had brought back to Pakistan many American toys including plastic guns and other military games. When they moved into a new rental house that was located a distance from other homes, the children had the toys strewn all over the floor where they had been playing with them during the day. That evening when Dr. Feroz and Mary went to their own bedroom they found one of the plastic guns on the floor. Without thinking about the nature of the toy, they picked it up and put it on the night table next to their bed for the evening. Then they retired for the night in their own bed. At about 2:00 a.m., some bandits begin breaking into the house through the master bedroom window that was just about ten feet away from the bed. As the bandits came through the window they looked around the room and saw the startled couple sitting up in bed and the "gun" on the table next to them. At that moment the bandit's leader decided that it would not be healthy for them to raid a house where the inhabitants owned American guns and they turned and fled the property.

For a moment Dr. Feroz did not understand why the bandits had left so abruptly until he turned his head and realized that the toy gun had scared them from robbing his house. It turned out to be a very lucky incident for the family because bandits can be very cruel and mistreat anyone that they rob. Dr. Feroz was thankful that the children did not put away their toys that night and it became a story that was told around the university often.

We never met any other Pakistani Christian families in Lahore, even though I was told there were an entire congregation and even a small Christian church. Of course, there were American and British Christians working in the embassies, the American hospital, and in international businesses who were living in Lahore. Dr. Feroz mentioned that he would sometimes take his family into the American compound to go to church on Sundays. Christians were treated as second class citizens, and in most Muslim countries forced to pay extra taxes for their beliefs. There were no Jews in Lahore that were Pakistani, although there might have been some foreign born Jews in banking or international business living there. If so, they kept to themselves and did not reveal their religious beliefs. During the 1947 partition of Pakistan and India, all Hindus and Sikhs were either killed or forced to immigrate to India.

During these winter days of 1969 Pakistan politics were very disturbing. The President at that time was a military man named Ayub Khan. The "Khan" family was descended from the elite soldier class of the Persian ruler who conquered Delhi in the 18th century. All people with the last name of "Khan" were supposed to be very militant and fierce. Khans are usually Punjabis with broad shoulders, very tall, and they moved up swiftly to high level positions in the army of Pakistan.

Ayub Khan became president of West Pakistan in 1958 after a military coup. He stayed in office until March 1969 when he resigned in favor of General Muhammad Yahya Khan who took over the government and installed martial law in Pakistan. There were riots and student processions throughout West Pakistan, and it became increasingly dangerous for me to be out in public or shopping in the bazaars. Ali was always avoiding the riot areas, and the university was closed several times to stop the students from wreaking any of the equipment or buildings. These were definitely strange times for Lahore, and I was getting bored just staying at home and listening to my one or two country western tapes.

I was receiving some letters from home, usually from my grandfather, Carl. He would write to me about his childhood in the small Missouri town where he grew up. These letters were my lifeline to my home and family. My sister would also write to me about her life in school and her many boyfriends. She told me about boxes of musical tapes that she had sent to me in Lahore, but after many months of waiting for them to arrive I realized that they had been stolen by someone. Mail was never delivered to our apartment. All of my letters and boxes had to be sent to Ali at the University of the Punjab. Ali would bring my letters home to me after he had read them first. I never suspected that he would read my mail before I received it or censor what type of letters I was getting from my family. After a while, I began to realize that Ali was suspicious of what family members might be writing to me concerning him. My mother was sure that I was being kept in seclusion, and she would write and ask me about my life in Lahore. I sent her stories concerning shopping trips and marriage ceremonies that we attended. I did not write to her about any of the difficult or troubling areas of my marriage or my life in Pakistan in order not to frighten her.

We had no phone in the house and even if we had decided to pay the high price of phone service to our apartment I could not afford to call America. During the entire stay of two years in Lahore I had no contact with my family by phone. If Ali wanted to make a phone call to someone in Lahore he would go to his office at the university or visit a friend who had a phone. As the months progressed, I began to feel very lonely and totally under the control of Ali, who would not allow me to do anything alone because of both safety reasons and his need to control my life. My days were spent reading books or washing my own clothes and waiting for Ali to come home so I might be able to go shopping or do something to break the monotony.

CHAPTER 12: INFIDELS IN LAHORE

Ali could sense that I was lonely for female companionship so when he met a young sophisticated Parsee girl at the University he told her all about his American wife. I was introduced to Barbara Adamjee outside Ali's classroom one day and we were immediately invited to her father's home for tea the next afternoon. Barbara was exactly my age and had recently been ordered home from Beirut, where she was attending the American University. Her father was a rich and powerful Parsee merchant and Barbara was his only daughter. She missed the cosmopolitan atmosphere of Beirut and was very lonely in Lahore. She had been born in Pakistan and could have anything she wanted because of her father's great wealth. But now she was home and her father was searching the Parsee community to try to introduce her to the proper man as possible husband material.

Parsees are the followers of Zoroaster and descendants of the ancient Persians who fled to India during the conquest of their own country by the Muslim Arabs in the 8th century. It is believed that the Magi from the east who came to worship at the birth of Jesus were probably Parsees from Persia. This religion is made up of interesting religious practices that are usually tolerant, generous, and wise. Parsees worship fire as the "son of God", a visible image of an invisible god. In every Parsee household there are numerous candles and receptacles for fires to be lit with ease. The Parsees are much more liberal in their treatment of women than any Muslim or Hindu family, so Barbara was a very liberal minded and a rather head strong young girl and was happy to find someone to talk to about her life.

Once we began our conversations with no men around, we had difficulty stopping our talks. All of my frustrations and observations about Muslim life poured out of me, and Barbara talked about her father trying to push her into marriage and forcing her return from Beirut because of the beginning hostilities in that region.

The next day at around 3:30 o'clock in the afternoon we drove to a large home in an expensive residential area of Lahore with green trees, gardens, canals, and high walls surrounding the house. I say house, but it was really closer to being a mansion. There were servants, gardeners, drivers, and body guards doing the everyday chores that are needed to maintain a mansion. The high walls surrounding the house were topped with glass shards imbedded in the concrete to ward off any bandits who might wish to climb over. Wealthy Pakistanis worried about kidnappers and bandits stealing their children.

We were admitted by a servant and shown into a large sitting room. There were no plastic coverings on furniture in this splendid house. Carved and ivory inlaid tables and chairs were arranged around the room with plenty of green potted plants. Gauze flowing white curtains were covering the French doors and a slight breeze pushed them into the room. The walls were a light peach color, and landscape paintings were hanging in various places around the room.

The ambience in the house was as if we had stepped into a home from a Victorian novel.

Suddenly Barbara burst into the room and asked us to sit down on one of the sofas. The servant was bringing in the tea and cookies and set the tray down in front of us on the coffee table. Barbara was giggling and talking rapidly and I could not hold back my thoughts for long. She was asking if I liked shopping, horseback riding, polo matches, dancing, American movies, and so many other things that I did not have much of a chance to ask her anything. We began pouring tea and passing the cookies around when Barbara's father entered the room. Ali and I were introduced to Mr. Adamjee, who was an extremely good looking, white haired man, with a handlebar mustache. He was a tall gentleman dressed in a white suit and striped vest. He shook hands all around and sat down near Barbara to have tea with us.

Ali and Mr. Adamjee talked about the political situation in the country as Barbara asked me if I wanted to see her bedroom. I gladly accepted and we swiftly walked out of the sitting room and away from the men who were engaged in deep discussion. Down a long hallway made of white marble was Barbara's large bedroom. As we talked about various topics she showed me her small attached sitting room and large bathroom with sunken tub. The bed in her room was a large four poster with elegant sheets and coverlet embroidered with delicate flowers. Her clothes were haphazardly lying around the room where she had obviously dropped them. I doubt she ever took care of any of her possessions because the household servants would follow her around and do it all for her. I was very jealous of the luxury bathroom, the likes of which I had never seen anywhere, including America. She had a real toilet, not two concrete foot pads over a hole, placed in the corner of the bathroom. A wide sink with marble counter top and a separate shower enclosed in light peach colored tiles were on one entire wall. The sunken tub was in the middle of the room and allowed Barbara to sit in bubble bath all day long if it pleased her. At the bottom of the tub the tiles were placed in the shape of a very round gold fish. Of course, there were gold faucets on all the fixtures. The walls of the bathroom were painted in murals out of Indian mythology. I was enchanted with the room and wanted, at that moment, nothing more than to live in her bathroom for the rest of my life.

We giggled and laughed about our lives and she invited me to go shopping with her and to have a drink of wine at the Intercontinental Hotel. It all sounded heavenly, but I had to ask Ali if I could accompany her to all these fun and interesting excursions. We walked back down the hall and to the room where the men were talking. I immediately blurted out that Barbara had asked me to accompany her shopping and snacking at the Intercontinental Hotel. The hotel was a fabulously high priced, four star luxury hotel where the English tourists hung out in the bar. Because Barbara was so wealthy and her father so powerful in business, Ali could not deny me this request in front of them, even though he was shocked by its nature. Ali believed shopping and drinking, without him accompanying us as chaperone, would be a rather wild and adventuresome day. In America no one would have thought twice about the adventure, but in Pakistan, Muslim women did not do this type of thing. So catching him off guard with my request forced him into quickly agreeing and displaying how open minded he was in this restrictive culture. Barbara said that she would send her driver to pick me up the next day at about 1:00 in the afternoon and we would have a terrific time. I was so excited I did not know what to do except smile and thank her for including me in this escapade.

We left the house after saying our goodbyes. I could not stop smiling about tomorrow's date. Ali was a little grumpy, but was at least encouraged that I would be fraternizing with an extremely wealthy heiress instead of just riff raff. When we returned to our apartment, Ali told his mother in Urdu what I was going to be doing the next afternoon and a reproachful look came over her face. She spoke some short Urdu sentences abruptly and looked over at me with a dark cloud over her face. I knew she did not approve of tomorrow's outing and was trying to tell Ali to stop me from going. But I also knew that Ali would not try to tell me that I could not go shopping with Barbara, mainly because of her father's wealth. Ali was trapped by his own greed and concern over having the wealthy family think badly of him. So I would finally get to have a little fun in this Muslim country.

The next day I dressed in my modern blue outfit which had tight pants and a blue silk chemise. The weather was clear and warm so I did not need a coat and Ali even gave me a little spending money for the shopping trip. Barbara's driver picked me up at exactly 1:00 in the afternoon and I was taken to Barbara's house. She was still getting dressed when I arrived, so I was shown into her bedroom by the maid. We talked about where to go while she was putting on a short skirt, long sleeve blouse, and white "go go" boots. She grabbed her purse and off we went in her chauffeured car to the gold bazaar.

Barbara spoke perfect Urdu and we had no trouble with vendors because we kept the driver with us as we shopped for gold jewelry. Barbara purchased a few bracelets made of 22 karat gold and put them on to wear home. I was not interested in gold, but began looking for things to take back with me to America when I returned. I found a jewelry box for my mother and some small silver jewelry pieces. Barbara did most of the shopping because she had plenty of money. The shop keepers were happy to see her and would ask us to enter their shops as we walked slowly down the rows of vendors.

We then went to a small grocery store so Barbara could pick up some American Instant Nescafe coffee. I was amazed that we could have purchased any food from America if we were ready to spend the very high prices at this import shop. Ali had not even told me some of these things were available in Lahore. A few more stops at the cloth and sari shops and we were ready for a drink and snacks at the Intercontinental Hotel.

It was about 4:00 in the afternoon by the time we drove up the regal entrance of the hotel and a door man opened the car door for us to get out. I could easily get used to this type of luxurious treatment, I told myself as we leisurely walked into the building.

We went straight to the hotel bar and sat at one of the tables. Soon a Pakistani waiter came over to the table to ask what we wanted to order. Barbara asked for a glass of red wine and I told the waiter I wanted the same thing. We also looked at the appetizer list on the menu and ordered some fried vegetable snacks and onion rings. It had been an interesting afternoon and we were both happy with our purchases; now it was the time to relax. I ended up having two glasses of wine before it was time to go home. We were both a little drunk by 5:30 p.m. Barbara was delivered home first and instructed the driver to take me to the apartment. Her driver dropped me off at the apartment about 6:00 p.m. and I went up stairs with my purchases.

I was still a little high with the wine and fun we had and did not think anyone would have reason to be upset with me. As I walked into the living room of the apartment Ali was seated on the sofa, reading a book. He asked what I had done all afternoon with Barbara and got very upset with me when I told him we finished up our day at the hotel bar drinking wine. He insisted that I not tell anyone about the wine and I agreed to keep quiet. He raised his voice and it was threatening and loud. Even though we both had a few alcoholic drinks in America, here in Pakistan it was considered rather risqué. Good Muslims don't drink any liquor, at least not in 1969, even though I found many instances in history books which talked about the Moghul emperors often addicted to wine and opium.

That weekend we received a note, delivered by the Adamjee driver, asking us to meet Mr. Adamjee and Barbara for dinner at the Hotel Intercontinental. Ali was flattered and of course we sent a note back with the driver saying we would meet them there at 7:00 that evening. His anger was suddenly over now that he could enjoy the wealthy Adamjee's hospitality, too. We dressed up, Ali in a suit and me in a sari, and drove over to the hotel in the Volkswagen. We were escorted to Mr. Adamjee's personal table in the dining room and were warmly greeted.

Mr. Adamjee and Barbara were charming and it calmed Ali's attitude toward these cosmopolitan people. Even he ordered a glass of wine so he would not appear to be too stuffy or overly religious. There was a dance band in the neighboring room and after dinner and drinks we danced a few slow dances to the music. Ali asked Barbara to dance and she accepted while I sat with her father talking about Pakistan's military politics. Everyone was very civilized and we all pretended we weren't living in an extremist Muslim country.

There were many other foreigners in the hotel restaurant and dance club. I heard several people speaking with French and English accents about what appeared to be business discussions, but I was never sure. Barbara did seem to blend in with a younger crowd and when the music picked up there were a group of young people dancing a very fast western dance on the dance floor. Her father kept a very sharp eye on her during the evening, and even though she was twenty feet away from him on the dance floor he knew who she was talking to or flirting with every minute. Later that evening we excused ourselves, thanked them for the dinner and left in our own car to drive back to the apartment.

In about a week or two we were invited to the local Polo club by Barbara and again picked up by their driver and taken to the Polo grounds. The club was a remnant from British rule in India and resembled country clubs in the States. We announced at the door that we were guests of Mr. Adamjee and were immediately escorted into the club. That afternoon was pleasant as we watched the polo matches from chairs on the club veranda shaded by brightly colored awnings. Mr. Adamjee owned several polo ponies and employed a rider who he paid to take care of them and play the game under his name. I think he was too old to be a polo player but probably enjoyed the game when he was a younger man.

During this afternoon Barbara asked me if I rode horses. I had ridden some as a young girl, but had never taken lessons or learned to ride an English saddle. I said I enjoyed riding, and Barbara and I decided to go horseback riding along the canal the next week. I worried about what to wear riding because I had not brought any riding pants or jeans with me to Pakistan. I also did not have the proper riding books and my sandals were rather skimpy. Barbara did have an extra pair of riding pants, but my feet were much bigger than her small size seven foot, so I was stuck with riding in simple shoes with heals.

I was picked up by the driver on the day of our riding adventure and taken to Barbara's home. Three horses were saddled with English saddles and standing in the garden quietly munching on the lawn. Barbara came out of the house to greet me and we were taken over to the horses by the riding master, also employed by Mr. Adamjee. Barbara had a little more experience with these horses and so she was helped up onto one particular horse. I was given a very calm horse and also helped up into the saddle by the riding master. The saddle felt like nothing was under me, it was so small and thin. I had only ridden on big western saddles but was game to give this adventure a try. It was decided that the three of us would ride down the canal and back again to the house for about thirty minutes. Everything went fine until on the way back Barbara put her horse into a canter and my horse decided to follow just as fast. I was unsteady and tried to slow the horse down when suddenly he stopped and I flew right over his head and landed on the ground. Luckily, the horse stopped in his tracks and waited for me to get mounted again. Barbara and the riding master were far ahead of me on the trail by this time, so I got up off the ground, dusted my pants off, and struggled back on the horse. We walked home slowly and arrived about ten minutes behind the other two riders. The riding master asked if I was all right, and I sheepishly murmured that everything was fine. I was very embarrassed that he somehow knew I had fallen from the horse, but he did not seem to mind. That was the last time Barbara asked me to go riding down the canal.

During one of my visits to Barbara's house I noticed that there were about twenty-five oil paintings of various sizes laid out along the dining room wall in a long row. I was fascinated with the paintings and carefully inspected each one. When Mr. Adamjee entered the room and found me examining the paintings he came over and asked me which ones I liked the best. I had spotted a large painting of an Indian woman whose eyes were very large, with almost a Modigliani-like Italian face. I kept returning to look at this particular painting several times and I told him I felt it was well done. I pointed to the painting and asked him about its history and who the artist had been. He said it was a young unknown man who was trying to get established. We started a conversation about art and he told me the history of several of the other paintings. Mr. Adamjee collected art and put it in several of his various homes around Pakistan. After our conversation Mr. Adamjee said that he would like to make a gift of the painting to me because it was a Parsee festival where they gave gifts, sort of like Christmas. I was overwhelmed with the gift and tried to refuse, but he insisted that I take it home. I finally accepted and the driver helped me get it to our apartment.

When Ali came home that afternoon from teaching, he was shocked to see the painting. Ali liked it at once, but his mother was not happy with it. Strict Muslims do not like depictions of people in their homes because they believe it is not correct to worship anyone but Allah. One will almost never see a painting such as this one hanging above a strict Muslim's fireplace. We hung the painting on the living room wall over a book case and enjoyed it very much, but Mahji would not sit near it or look at it because she felt it was sacrilegious. I made Ali promise that he would ship the painting to America when we returned to live in the States. It was too beautiful to leave with his family who would have sold it immediately for anything they could get for it.

I was allowed to see Barbara as often as I liked and was picked up by the driver many times to be taken to her home and just hang around and talk with her. Once when I was there I saw piles of gold rings and necklaces sitting out in the open on a table and was told by Barbara that her father had brought the jewelry home for gifts to family members. There had to be a significant amount of money spent on that jewelry because I saw diamonds, emeralds, and rubies set in the 22 karat gold. The last time the driver took me home before I left the country, he asked me to give him a present as a parting gift. I was taken totally by surprise, because I knew he was paid very well by Mr. Adamjee. I inquired what sort of present he wanted and he said he would like to have my watch. I did not know what to say so I just kept quiet. When we got to the apartment I immediately left the car and ran up the steps without commenting to the driver about his request. I told Ali what the driver had said and he was not surprised. He said he would give the driver a small gift of money next time he saw him. I guess it was traditional to compensate servants when they had been so often relied upon for a particular service.

CHAPTER 13: THE WIFE OF A FRIEND

On a warm, sunny day in the spring of 1969, Ali's friend Shahji came rushing into the apartment in the early afternoon. I was reading a novel in my bedroom and Babur and Mahji were sitting in the living room, Mahji praying and Babur studying. Shahji was out of breath because he had run up the steps to the apartment and burst in through the kitchen door. He started talked very hurriedly in Urdu and then changed to English as I came into the room. He had a very unusual request for me. "Will you go to the American Hospital with me so that we can get my cousin's wife admitted?" My immediate response was to ask what was wrong with her that she needed to go to a hospital. Shahji said that his cousin's wife had not been feeling well for days and had an extremely painful headache and backache. She moaned from pain and fainted at home so her husband rushed her to a Lahore women's hospital, The Fatima Jinnah Hospital.

Upon arrival at this medical facility she had been assigned to a small cot and placed in a hallway outside a women's ward until a female doctor could visit her. Several days had passed and this poor woman had not been moved into a ward or even examined by a doctor. She was delirious and moaning from pain in the hallway and being ignored by all the hospital staff. Her mother was sitting next to her cot on the floor and providing her water to drink while she lay ill. Her mother also had to carry this young woman to the bathroom several times per day. The woman's husband was not allowed to visit her because she was so close to the hospital's female ward, where women might not be totally veiled, but lying in small beds in a long row. So her mother would leave her position at the cot and go outside the hospital to tell the husband of his wife's condition. As her illness worsened, her husband decided to find Shahji and ask him to help get his wife admitted to the American hospital in Lahore. The woman's husband had hired an ambulance to pick up his wife and transport her across the city to the American hospital's emergency room.

I had brought with me from America a medical encyclopedia that allowed me to look up the disease symptoms and try to identify it. As Shahji was telling the story to me, I found my encyclopedia and began quickly leafing through the pages looking for the woman's symptoms. Suddenly I came across the word MENINGITIS, the inflammation of the meninges of the brain and spinal cord. I also read that it could be very contagious in some forms of the disease. I read the description of the sickness aloud to Shahji and he was very surprised that I could diagnose this woman's problem. At that moment I decided that I must do what I could to help this woman receive appropriate treatment or she might die.

I told Shahji that I would go with him to the American hospital, but could not necessarily guarantee that she would be admitted. I promised I would try to convince the hospital staff that she needed to be treated immediately. So Shahji directed Babur to go to the university and explain to Ali what we were doing for his cousin's wife. He gave Babur a few rupees to pay for a cab ride to the university campus so he could get to Ali rapidly.

Shahji and I ran downstairs and I suddenly stopped short in surprise. I had assumed that he had taken a cab ride to our home, but instead I found parked outside of our door was a small motorcycle that Shahji used for transportation to his workplace. I had ridden once on my brother's large motorcycle in Carbondale, Illinois, but this one was a very small Japanese model and it looked rather dangerous. Shahji assured me he would drive carefully and that he carried passengers on the back often. He jumped on the motorcycle and started the motor while I watched with alarm. I tied my long scarf around my head and neck and decided to take the chance that I might be killed in a crash between motorcycle and bus. I was nervous, but I carefully mounted the motorcycle behind Shahji and grabbed him around the waist. This was rather risqué for Pakistan, but I think Shahji enjoyed it, and I felt safer holding on to him rather than trying to hold onto the sides of the small seat.

I had never seen the American hospital and was a little surprised that one existed in Lahore. As we flew across town on the small motorcycle I was trying to think of what I would say to a hospital administrator about the cousin's wife, who I had never met. The hospital was near the American Embassy and as we approached the large white building I noticed the sign on the front door. "United Christian Hospital" was where we were going to try and admit this Muslim woman. I did not say anything to Shahji, a devout Shiite Muslim who would not ever think of associating with Christians in his everyday life, but in this emergency looked toward a Christian institution that was supposed to be the best in town.

We sped up the large concrete drive way leading to the emergency room of the hospital and stopped at the front door. I got off the motorcycle and went into the wide double door of the main building. A modern, clean information desk was immediately in the front door, the floors were shining, and everything looked clean and antiseptic. I pulled my scarf down off my hair and approached the woman at the front desk. I asked the woman behind the desk, in English, who to talk to about getting a woman in an extreme emergency admitted to the hospital. The woman referred me to a doctor down the hall way by pointing her finger.

I ran down the hall and started talking to a doctor about the ambulance that was on its way from the Fatima Jinnah Hospital. I told him the symptoms and ask him to look at her because I felt it was a life or death situation for this poor suffering woman. At that moment the ambulance arrived at the hospital emergency room and the woman was taken out and wheeled into a small cubicle surrounded by plastic curtains hanging on metal rods. Two Pakistani female nurses and two American doctors immediately began to examine the woman and question her spouse, who had come with her in the ambulance, about her symptoms. I was standing about 10 feet away from the cubicle and could see what was happening through a slit in the curtains. The doctors seemed to be very thorough and checked her blood pressure, temperature, and started an I.V. for fluids and pain control.

Shahji and I were then escorted to the lobby to wait for information about the woman. At that time Ali walked into the hospital and spotted us waiting in the lobby. Shahji told him the entire story and asked his forgiveness for stealing his wife in such a hurry. Of course Ali trusted Shahji entirely and we all sat down to wait for news from the emergency room doctors.

After an hour, the husband of the woman came out of the emergency room and started talking to Shahji in Urdu. The man did not speak any English and was visibly shaken by the entire experience. The woman had been diagnosed with Meningitis and was going to be immediately admitted to the hospital. She would be put in a ward with other women and her mother could stay to watch and help take care of the woman. She would recover, I was told, but might have some brain damage because of the swelling and the time lapsed before real treatment had been given to her.

Ali and I decided to leave the hospital at that time and walked out to the parking lot to get into the Volkswagen and drive back to the apartment. Shahji stayed at the hospital to help the family get things settled and to bring anything they might need.

I had experienced the difference between the average Pakistani hospital and the Christian/American healthcare system in Pakistan, and felt very sorry for people who were forced to visit the Pakistani hospitals. Having been raised in America, I did not think about the status of health care around the world, and now I was being shown a slice of what people in third world countries experience every day. Previously I had thought that because the British had ruled India and Pakistan for hundreds of years their medical system would be much more up to date. But now I realized that medicine probably had not advanced much since the British left India in 1947, and might have even deteriorated in this Muslim country.

Approximately one month later I asked Shahji how his cousin's wife was doing and he told me that she was home still recovering from her ordeal. In this country, when people got very sick it was the custom to cut off all their hair. The theory behind this practice was to insure their strength would be directed toward their illness and facilitate a speedy recovery. I never met the woman and only briefly met her husband on the day we took her to the hospital. No one ever told me anything about her recovery from this serious disease and I always felt that they were hiding something about her true health status. I felt that she would have been admitted to this Christian facility even if I had not been there to speak for her. It astonished me to see that everyone else involved believed that without me at the hospital the sick woman would have been turned away.

This experience underscored for me how much the Pakistani Muslims did not understand about American/Christian charity or empathy for others. I suspect that Shahji's family was mentally transferring what would have happened at one of their own hospitals in this situation. Women and children in Pakistan are not treated with respect or humanity, and it was a surprise to me that the husband did not leave his wife at the first hospital to die in the hallway. She might have recovered on her own, but who knows how terribly painful her recovery would have been. The pain and related after effects of Meningitis can be extreme because of the swelling of the brain and other tissues surrounding her spinal cord. Shahji's cousin's family was not rich or well educated. The wife was lucky to be alive and related to Shahji in this particular instance. I often wondered if the husband, Shahji's cousin, actually felt some love for his wife to have taken so much effort and trouble to insure her well being.

During the spring of 1969 I had noticed that some people had small dogs as pets, so I asked Ali about getting a puppy. Ali laughed and said that most Pakistani's hated dogs because they were so filthy. Cats were universally hated and I never saw anything but feral cats in the old walled city. Children usually threw rocks at these cats even though they were catching mice and keeping the place a little healthier. He would not let me touch any dog we saw or request a puppy. I found out that most of these pet dogs were from India or China and were expensive if you wanted to purchase a pure bred Tibetan terrier.

I complained to Shahji one day about not having a pet and he suggested that they try to find me a baby mongoose. He had wild stories about pet mongooses sleeping with children who tamed them. He said he knew some people that found them occasionally and trained them to become wonderful pets. Ali did not seem to be upset about a baby mongoose, at least not while I was in the room, but I was never given one as a pet. Sometimes Shahji said he was trying to find me one, but it never materialized. However, one day Ali came home with a green parrot in a wire cage. This was exciting and I put it on the back porch off our bedroom. The parrot made lots of noise, and when I tried to touch it or train it, he bit me hard with his beak. This parrot was truly wild. Sometimes it would squawk so loudly that the neighbors would complain about the noise. I had seen many of these green parrots in the bazaars of Lahore where vendors would have twenty or thirty in a large cage to sell to customers. I never saw a trained bird in anyone's home. It would have been so much nicer to have a singing canary or finch, but Ali would not let me pick out my own pet.

After a month of hearing the green parrot screech and bite my fingers, I took it to the edge of the porch and opened the cage door. It flew happily to a nearby large tree and then out of my sight. I had freed it because it was totally wild and I felt it was not right to keep it locked up in a cage. When Ali came home that night I told him that I had freed the parrot and he said that he would not buy me another one or any other pet. The parrot had cost about fifty rupees and now Ali felt he had wasted money on me. I was disappointed, but felt good about the parrot's freedom and decided that I was not going to beg for any other pets in this country.

CHAPTER 14: CELEBRATION

Late one afternoon Ali came home and told me to change clothes into something nicer because we were driving to the old walled city to visit someone. I changed into a silk chemise and silk pajama pants and we headed out in the Volkswagen to visit this mysterious un-named friend. As usual, we parked near one of the large gates to the walled city and walked in over narrow cobblestone streets.

When we arrived at the specific house he knocked at the door and Ali spoke in Urdu to the man who answered the door. He introduced me to this man and I gave the proper greetings. I still had no idea why we were here talking to this person whom I had never met. The man invited us into his house and we walked upstairs to his study. Ali asked me to wait in a sitting room while he talked to the gentleman alone. Tea was brought to me by a young boy and I sat looking out the window while Ali and the man went into his study to talk. After about thirty minutes Ali and the man came back into the room and invited me into the study also.

It was then that I learned this man was the professor grading my University of the Punjab tests for my Bachelors degree. It had been about four months since I took the tests and now I was here to see the results. The man pulled out my test booklet from a large stack of papers and showed my scores clearly marked in blue ink. I had made one hundred sixteen points on the English Language section out of a possible two hundred points. In English Literature I had scored one hundred three points out of a possible 200 points. My Indo-Pakistani History score was one hundred sixteen points out of two hundred possible, and the optional general studies portion I had scored sixty points out of a possible one hundred points. These all appeared to me like really low scores, but it turned out to be over 55% of the possible perfect score, and that allowed me to pass the tests. I had squeaked by in my Bachelor of Arts examination of 1969 and would be receiving an official degree in several months.

I do not know if Ali paid the gentleman who scored my exam to give me a better grade, but they were in the room talking for at least 30 minutes before I was asked to join them. I suspect that Ali did give him a gift of money for allowing us to visit and see the test results. I was happy with these test results and did not care how I had passed the exams. Later in life these simple scores allowed me to enter graduate school and complete a Master's degree in education. Of course, at the time I had no idea how this experience would help my future career.

We left the house after offering profuse thanks to the gentleman and decided to celebrate by having dinner at the Tanduri chicken restaurant in downtown Lahore. I was never introduced to this simple professor again or taken to his home. What really happened that afternoon was always kept a secret from me and I have often wondered if the truth was any different than the scene I witnessed in this man's home.

Approximately one month later Mahji was called away from our apartment to immediately travel to the old city and stay at Salim's home. His big fat wife, Bahji, whom he always fought with in front of everyone, was about to give birth to their twelfth child. I was surprised to learn that she was even pregnant again. I had seen her several times during the last nine months, but she was so fat that it was impossible to say that she was pregnant or not. I had always heard from Ali that Salim despised his wife and that he was going to divorce her someday and find a new, younger wife. This particular situation appeared to contradict everything I had heard so often from Ali, and the truth was that Salim was just unable to keep his hands off his wife. It might be a little difficult to divorce a woman who has given you eleven boys during your eighteen year marriage.

The baby was due any day now and Mahji must be at their home to help with the birth. Salim's wife would not be going to a hospital to have her child. Instead of a doctor or hospital, a midwife would be hired and brought into the house to insure a good delivery of the child. Two days later we received word about the birth from Babur's younger brother Siyanda. He arrived by bus to let us know that all was well with Salim's wife and the new baby was another son. I'm sure that young Fozia had prayed for a little sister, but instead here was the eleventh boy for the family. Of course, all in the neighborhood were celebrating and we were invited to visit and see the baby boy. Baby boys in

Islam are circumcised very quickly after birth and it is celebrated with boxes of sweets for the mother and family. We drove to the old walled city, parked the Volkswagen, and walked to Salim's home. We made sure to pick up some very delectable sweets and sugar cookies at the bakery before we got to the house.

Inside Salim's home we found several older women, including Mahji, attending to a very uncomfortable Bahji. A dirty, toothless old woman all dressed in black stood in the corner of the room. I was told this woman was the midwife who helped bring the little boy into the world. The mother of the child, Bahji, was lying on a char pi bed to the side of the room, all dressed up in a brocade gold and blue outfit. Her head was resting on her arm, eyes closed, while moans issued from her fat lips. Bahji's hair was done neatly in an oily bun, pulled back from her large round face. She obviously wanted as much sympathy as she could possibly gain from her pose.

I could not imagine her giving birth in this particular outfit she was wearing and asked Ali about her fancy clothes. He told me that she had changed clothes immediately after the birth so that when all the family visited she would be dressed for the celebration. The tiny baby boy was resting on his back across the room in a small basket with a blanket under him. Mahji was sitting near him saying her rosary beads in prayers for his well being. He could not have weighed more than five pounds and was crying loudly to be fed by his mother. He did not have a diaper on his bare little pink bottom and as we entered the room a stream of urine issued from his little penis. Mahji picked up a cloth diaper and placed it over his little body to catch the stream. The one day old baby already had black kohl painted on his new born black eye lids. His eyes were dripping tears and yells issued forth from his well formed lungs. He certainly appeared to be a strong little boy to me.

I did not ask to pick him up because the baby was not wearing diapers, although he did have a tiny shirt made of gold and red brocade cloth. Maybe his screams were due to the scratchy cloth his mother and grandmother had dressed him in on his first day of life. He was born the evening before with all the women in the family surrounding the mother, helping in every way they could. Even young Fozia was allowed to watch the birth of her new brother, a good way to teach the facts of life to a young girl.

The room was filled with incense smelling of jasmine and I thought, at the time, that it might be to kill the smell of dirty bodies and blood. Ali's brother Salim was in the other room offering tea and cakes to all his distant relatives who were dropping by the house to see the new son. We decided to sit with Salim and talk to the visitors instead of hanging around the birthing suite. Later that evening we returned to our own home and did not visit the baby again for several weeks.

Mahji stayed for eight days taking care of the mother and son in their house in the old walled city. We were asked to pick her up when she was ready to return to the apartment and so drove the Volkswagen to that area of town. Before Mahji was ready to go with us she asked to take me to visit a woman who was a famous religious mystic. I thought this might be an interesting experience and I agreed to go with her to this mystic's house, which was located about three city blocks away from Salim's. I was dressed in an orange and white sari and sandals because the weather was beginning to get quite warm. Mahji put on her black burkah and, holding my hand, led the way to the house. Mahji did not speak any English so I just followed closely trying not to get separated from her.

We arrived at the woman's house and gently knocked on the door. Immediately the door was opened by a woman clothed in a black burkah. We were shown through the old wooden door, and as I entered the room I was surprised to see the room filled with at least thirty women. They were all sitting on oriental rugs placed on the floor around an older woman who had the holy Qur'an open before her on a wooden book holder. Mahji introduced me to the woman and I said the proper Muslim greeting to her. Mahji explained to the mystic that I had converted to Islam when I was married to her son, Ali. A younger woman next to me turned around and asked in English if it was true that I had converted to Islam. I answered her that I had done so at my wedding.

The female mystic was friendly and gestured for me to come across the rug close to where she was sitting in front of the Qur'an. As I approached her, I bent my head and she raised her hands to my hair to whisper several prayers over me. Mahji repeated the prayers in a slow and quiet voice, but I was never told what they were praying about. Later I learned from Ali that this mystic was given money every time she prayed for someone. The Muslim women who attended the mystic's Qur'an reading sessions she held in her home always brought money with them. They supported her because they believed she had some special mystic qualities of piety and worked miracles through her prayers. I suppose she had a certain amount of success because women kept coming to her home for lots of repeat business. For the very short time I was in her home I saw at least ten additional women enter the front door and ask for special prayers to be said for their families.

As Mahji and I left the building she dropped some rupees into a wooden box near the door. This is how the mystic woman made her living, and it appeared to be a good living from the size of the house and the oriental rugs covering the floors. We both walked swiftly back to Salim's home and then Ali drove us back to our apartment.

Maybe the blessings were for a safe trip back to America, because within a few days I received a letter from my Grandmother Quinn. She informed me that she would pay for my trip back to America if I would meet her in London and act as her escort for a short tour of Ireland, Scotland, and the Netherlands before we returned to the United States. She gave me tentative dates for the trip and I was supposed to write her back immediately about my decision. I was desperate to leave Pakistan and this was the perfect way out, without causing anyone offence. So I begged Ali to let me tell my grandmother I would meet her in London in early May 1969.

Ali said it was fine, even though he could not leave for America for another six months. I would return to the United States, live with my parents, find a job, and wait for him to join me in six months. Leaving earlier would allow me to miss the coming hot weather and monsoon season in Lahore. I was relieved when the arrangements were agreed upon and I wrote that evening to my grandmother so she could purchase both of our tickets for the trip.

I was unhappy with my life in Pakistan. My husband was overbearing, controlling, and not romantic. Our sex life was unsatisfying for me and I was having second thoughts about a life with this man and wanted to return to America to think over my future. I felt his family was extremely backward and uneducated, and I did not like the way women were treated in his country. The trip to London was a perfect excuse to leave early, without Ali.

The trip to the British Isles and America was being planned and paid for by my maternal grandmother and grandfather. I was told later that my Grandfather, Carl had sold Walt Disney stock to pay for the trip expenses. I just had to decide what presents I was taking with me and what was being sent in boxes to America. I went shopping several times in the Lahore bazaars to find the right items to bring with me in my suitcases. I still had some western style clothes that I had brought with me and not worn in Pakistan. I could buy extra clothes and other personal items in London with my grandmother.

I was forced to promise a visit to Ali's older sister, Shafia, and her family who all lived in Newcastle Upon Tyne Four. So I asked my grandmother to make the tickets to England to include a trip to this small northern English town. I did not really want to visit this branch of the family but felt that I must accept Ali's wishes in this matter. The tickets were sent to me and the time was approaching when I would leave Lahore forever.

CHAPTER 15: RETURN TO THE WEST

May 2nd was the day for my return trip to begin. I was to catch a flight from Lahore to Karachi, and then London, early in the morning. I had been packing for several weeks and deciding what to do with the items I was leaving behind in Lahore and did not want to take back to the United States. I gave Babur all of my country western music tapes because he loved to listen to the songs. Fozia received all of my Pakistani clothes except two heavily brocaded silk saris that I was bringing back with me. The silk was too fine and luxurious to leave with Ali's relatives, and I wanted my mother to see the beauty of these fabrics. I packed my American dresses, shoes, and other items that would be appropriate for the trip with my grandmother. Other items were put in boxes to be mailed back to America. Ali and I visited several of our Pakistani friends before I left so that I could say goodbye to them. Ali's friend, Shahji, came often to the apartment before May and visited with me to extract promises that I would not forget his family.

The two weeks before I was to leave Lahore turned into a whirlwind of activities as I tried to prepare for the coming trip. Ali and I decided that it would be best for me to take the twenty-two karat gold bangles, ruby ring, and gold earrings with me on this trip, instead of having him attempt to bring it into the United States in six months. He believed that I would be more likely not to be given trouble at customs with the expensive gold jewelry. If I was stopped entering the United States with the jewelry, he expected my grandmother would pay the customs fine for me. Ali gave me approximately two hundred dollars in American money so that I would be able to purchase a roundtrip train ticket from London to Newcastle to visit his sister. I also needed cab fare to get from the London train station to the elite hotel in Langham Place, W-1, where my grandmother was going to meet me.

Early in the morning on May 2nd, I awoke at 5:00 o'clock in the morning to prepare for the long trip. My excitement about getting out of Pakistan and leaving this restrictive society was greater than my anticipated joy of seeing my grandmother again. I felt as if I was running away from my demons rather than running toward something beloved. I dressed in a very comfortable sari and heavy sweater for the plane trip, believing that it would be best for me to arrive at Shafia's home in Newcastle in Pakistani clothes. I also considered not letting Mahji see me leave Pakistan dressed in my American short skirts and high heeled shoes. My menstrual period had started the day before and it was a secret pleasure for me to realize that I was not pregnant with Ali's child. It also prevented Ali from trying to make love to me before I left Pakistan. Muslims would not have sex with a woman who was menstruating. I had barely turned twenty-one years old in January and did not want any children at this time in my life. My problem with having the menstrual period was the inconvenience of traveling in a sari and trying to change my tampons during the flight or on my train trip to Shafia's home at Newcastle. I was alone and could not leave my luggage or be stuck in a bathroom in the airport or train station and risk theft of my belongings. I would just have to do the best I could, and if it meant bleeding on my clothing, then that was what would happen on the long trip.

Ali would not go with me to the airport; instead I took a cab ride alone. Ali said he had an important meeting at the university that morning and he could not get away to drive me and then wait for the plane to leave. I did not care about this situation and was happy to make the parting short and sweet at the apartment instead of long and drawn out at the airport. My mind was already miles away from Pakistan and now I needed to actually leave the country as soon as I could.

Ali loaded my luggage into the cab while Mahji said prayers over my head and kissed my face many times. She was blessing my trip and praying for a speedy return to their family in Pakistan. I reluctantly kissed Ali a very short goodbye and got into the back seat of the cab. As the cab pulled away from the apartment, I relaxed into the middle of the back seat cushion and I knew instantly that I would never return to this country in my lifetime. It was a clear choice I was silently making and I repeated it to myself several times over on the way to the airport. It became a secret promise that I made to myself for the future. This was the last few minutes I would be living in this country. I was sure of this particular wish more than I have ever been sure of any resolution in my life.

At the Lahore airport I swiftly went though boarding procedures and walked confidently onto a British Airways 707 jet plane. At last I was free from Islamic conventions and laws and could mentally transform back into my American self once again. I just had one more official family visit to make and that was in Newcastle upon Tyne Four, Shafia's house. This time I was not nervous as the plane lifted off the runway in Lahore. A short, two hour stops in Karachi for a passport check and I was on my way to London, England. I could not help smiling to myself the entire way to England and did not feel afraid or unsure for one moment. I had endured what was necessary in Pakistan and now I was returning to my former life of being an emancipated American girl. I could barely wait to experience normal American living such as real toilet seats, bath tubs and showers, kitchen stoves, hamburgers, speaking to anyone I pleased, wearing short skirts, jeans and rough clothes, and not asking permission to go shopping at a store or market.

I arrived at London's Heathrow Airport late in the afternoon of that same day. I was able to fall asleep for short naps on the plane flight from Karachi so I was rested and ready to get through customs and find the train station. Now I was fearless! Nothing was going to hold me back from seeing my beloved grandmother in a few days time. I just needed to visit Ali's sister and very quickly return to London to find the hotel where she would meet me.

My choice of wearing the sari was a big mistake. I should have dressed as an American girl from the moment I left Lahore. In England, individuals from India or Pakistan were discriminated against because of their history as a "colony" of Britain. I was a blond American girl, dressed in a sari, arriving from Pakistan. The cloth was cumbersome and made it difficult to carry my luggage and get through customs. The customs official, dressed in a British uniform, glared at my passport, asked me questions, and searched my luggage very carefully for something I did not have. At the time I was not aware that young people were trying to smuggle drugs from India and Pakistan and that anyone from those countries was suspect and thoroughly searched.

I finally got through customs and immediately found a cab stand outside the airport. As I entered the large black cab, I asked for Victoria Train Station and immediately the cabbie sped off in a hurry.

The Victoria Station ticket office sold me a round trip ticket to Newcastle upon Tyne Four for the high speed train trip for about $75.00. I was helped with my luggage onto the train and soon was speeding toward the north of England. My tampon was leaking onto my underpants and I was nervous about leaving my luggage to go to the bathroom. After a short time on the moving train modesty forced me to find the bathroom and change my tampon. I still was ecstatic that this menstrual period proved I was free of pregnancy and, even though inconvenient, it was good to have this simple assurance of freedom.

It was about 9:00 o'clock at night when the train arrived in the station at Newcastle. I gathered my luggage, disembarked from the train, and found a cabbie who would take me to the address, 186 Dilston Road, Newcastle Upon Tyne 4. I was reminded of the old British saying, "bringing coal to Newcastle" as the taxi sped through the town. The town was an old coal mining area and every house had smoke stacks with coal dust coloring the buildings gray. Approximately thirty minutes later the cab pulled up in front of a dark two story row house in a poor section of town. I paid the cabbie, got my luggage, and went to the front doorway of the small house. The door bell sounded loudly as I waited for someone to respond to my intrusion.

In a few minutes a young girl, about sixteen years old came to the door. "Aunt Layla?" she inquired as I looked at her. I forced a smile and nodded my head. Was this my niece, Shafia's daughter? She invited me into the house and there was much celebration and excited talking. I was introduced to Ali's sister Shafia, her husband, Ahmed, and their son and daughter. Later they showed me my small bedroom and I prepared for sleep at 11:00 p.m. that evening. I had not realized how very tired I was after having traveled thousands of miles in this one day, from Lahore to northern England. I did not take a shower, but just put on pajamas to sleep in and dropped upon the twin sized bed totally exhausted. My big day was over and now I could look forward to the future. In slightly more than 24 hours I would see my Grandmother Quinn and my long ordeal ended. Life would return to normal and I could, once again, resume my American identity.

The next morning I was awakened by Shafia, a meek but heavy set woman of about 45 years of age. I came downstairs in my robe and pajamas and had a hot cup of tea with cream for breakfast. Shafia made eggs and toast for me to eat, and her daughter asked me questions because she, Shafia, could not speak English.

Later I took a shower and changed to western clothes to have a tour around town with my sixteen year old niece. We visited a local museum and walked to some old stone churches and talked like western girls only five years apart in age will do. This Pakistani girl had been raised most of her life in northern England and was western in all her habits, dress and thinking. Her main concern as she grew older was that her parents would take her back to Pakistan and force her to marry a cousin who was probably not as liberal or educated as herself.

I had met many of her male cousins in Pakistan and she was right, they were all living in the old walled city and had not advanced in school very far. I felt bad for her and sorry about her future, but only she could change it by rebelling while still in England. She was far too obedient a daughter to run away or insist on attending college in this northern English town. She felt trapped and helpless, knowing that she must do as her parents told her. Totally controlled by circumstances of her life and heritage from her Muslim tradition, she knew what her life would be like in Pakistan.

Another alternative for her, of course, would have been for her father and mother to find an equally educated young Muslim man currently living and attending school in England. But this family was too traditional, and her father had already begun preliminary talks about marriage to his brother's sons in Pakistan. Shafia had married her own first cousin and now her daughter must do the same thing in a few years' time. Apparently there was no alternative way of life for her.

That night Shafia cooked a family dinner for us and I went to bed early. The next morning I quickly packed, dressed myself in American clothes, and said my goodbyes to the family. A taxi was called and soon I was being driven to the Newcastle Railroad Station. At 10:00 in the morning I boarded the train to London. My anticipation at seeing my grandmother was uppermost in my mind. After a three hour trip I arrived at Victoria Station in London and took my luggage off the train to a taxi stand. A taxi was hailed for me and I was on my way to the St. George Hotel in Langham Place, W-1.

The hotel was at the end of Regent Street and occupied the top six floors of a sixteen story building, with a ground floor entrance. As the taxi stopped in front, I saw a uniformed doorman open the taxi door. My driver brought my two suitcases to the doorman who immediately hailed a porter to carry the luggage. I paid the taxi driver and followed the porter bearing my luggage into the main lobby of the hotel. At the registration desk I asked if my grandmother had checked into the hotel yet and was told she was having tea in the sitting room next to the lobby. I immediately turned away from the registration desk and walked swiftly toward the sitting room about fifty feet away. My eyes were sweeping the room anxiously, and as I walked I suddenly saw the woman I wanted to see more than anyone else in the world.

There, seated in a high backed chair was my Grandmother Quinn. Her hair was white, her smiling face was very round, and caring, and I found myself crying as I rushed into her warm, waiting arms. We both kissed and hugged and laughingly talked very fast. I felt I was finally safe and at home with this woman's arms around me, standing in an English hotel lobby. Now I could begin a new life as an independent woman and not be controlled by Muslim customs and men. I was with my beloved grandmother who had rocked me as a child and whispered that I was smart and strong. I was home. Mentally and emotionally changes had taken place within me during that brief moment of finding my Grandmother Quinn and holding tight to her. Once again I was a free American woman with no Islamic chains to bind me or a religion I did not believe in or wish to follow. Now I was free to live, dress, talk, eat, and feel what I wanted, not at the mercy of some Muslim man. It was May 4th, 1970; a beautiful, sunny, clear day in London.

CHAPTER 16: IT'S NOT OVER

The two weeks traveling in the British Isles was interesting and took my mind off the last eighteen months in Pakistan. Grandma Quinn and I stayed in the same hotel rooms together and I told her some of my stories, but mainly kept the items that I knew would upset her secret. She only heard about the adventures and how interesting Pakistan was, and she was fascinated by the jewelry and fabrics that I had brought back with me. Quinn was very happy to hold these foreign items, look at them and wonder about the places she would never visit.

We returned to St. Louis in late May 1970, where the entire family was waiting to deliver us to my parents' new apartment in Kirkwood. During the time I had been in Pakistan, father had taken a new job in a suburb of St. Louis and mother had gotten a teaching job in a high school in Kirkwood. They had sold the house in Carbondale and moved to an apartment in Kirkwood where they could take their time searching for a new home to purchase.

We arrived in the early evening and my sister, brother, and other family had dinner ready while I related stories of my life in Lahore. I told them all that Ali had to stay in Pakistan for several more months and then he would be coming to join me. In the interim I would find a job, live with my parents in their spare bedroom, and begin saving money for Ali's return trip to America.

I did not tell them of my doubts about my marriage because that would be announcing that they had been right all along. I was hiding my true feelings and pretending that all was well between Ali and me. Maybe this was false hope and I was mistaken in believing I could live a normal life with this man. I was sure that as soon as he came to America he would adopt our values and way of life. I should have filed for divorce at that very moment, but was too stubborn to admit that my parents and grandparents had been right.

After a week of rest and shopping for new clothes, I began looking for a job. Located very near my parents apartment was a small community college. Because I had worked in a library during my Southern Illinois University experience and in the Lahore American School in Pakistan, I decided to check out the college and see if the library needed an employee. I was hired immediately as a secretary who would file books, type letters, and give students directions. My boss was an older woman who ran the library and the audiovisual department of the college.

For several months I worked in this position and enjoyed interacting with students approximately my own age. I told everyone about my husband who would be joining me very soon from Pakistan. In those days there was only astonishment about this Middle Eastern country half way around the world; no one feared terrorists or extremist Muslims. The world was innocent of suicide bombings, and even Pakistan had not experienced this type of violence.

In September I was able to send Ali the money for his ticket to America. He arrived in St. Louis in early October and my grandparents drove up from Cape Girardeau to welcome him back. During our reunion that evening he proceeded to yell at my Grandmother so much that it made her cry. I was in the kitchen at the moment this interchange was taking place, but when I found out what had happened I was shocked and upset. It turned out that my grandmother was telling Ali how she and my grandfather had worked for everything they now owned in America and Ali became offended. He believed she was instructing him, a Muslim man, about not depending upon his wife's relatives to support him. He stormed out of the room and sulked in the bedroom leaving my grandmother in tears.

I will never forget watching my grandparents drive away – headed back to Cape Girardeau, my grandmother's face was half hidden with a handkerchief. She would not have offended anyone for any reason and did not understand the difference in cultures that made Ali yell at her in a very offensive way. I did my best to explain to Ali that she did not mean to offend him but was just telling him a little about her life. Ali took weeks to get over this offense. He lied to my parents by saying to them that the incident was nothing to him, but in our bedroom he told me how much he hated my grandmother.

Within two weeks Ali was looking for a job around Kirkwood and other St. Louis suburbs and applied for an opening as director of the communications department at the community college where I worked. He was interviewed by several top officials and hired within a month. I had to quit work because of a rule at the college that two people in the same family could not work within the same department. The communications department controlled the library and Ali began reporting to the same woman that I had reported to when I held my position there. I had no reason to believe that having a woman boss would cause any trouble for Ali, but it did very quickly.

After Ali had his job, I started looking for an apartment that we could move into and move out of my parents' home. It was easy to find a two bedroom place near the college campus. We rented it, moved in, and began purchasing furniture within two months. I had already purchased a small Volkswagen Beetle and was making payments on it because of my earlier secretary job. My father had co-signed for my car purchase, so we had a car and an apartment in which to live.

After we moved into the apartment, Ali would fight with me about being unemployed and staying home. I decided to continue my education and enrolled in the university that was north of Kirkwood. I could not take graduate classes because they would accept only a few course hours from my degree at the University of the Punjab. So I enrolled in undergraduate classes which interested me, such as anthropology, French, English, and history. Slowly I began building hours to complete an American undergraduate degree.

In late spring 1971, Ali put pressure on me to start a family with him and have his children. He wanted me to get pregnant. I was barely 22 years old and really did not want to begin having children. I was not happy living with Ali, our home life was very depressing, and he gambled several times a week with friends he found. These gambling trips left me home alone to watch television or study. He often brought home large handfuls of cash which he had won by cheating at cards. These card games left me cold, and I knew he was winning by cheating the men that he had found to associate with during the evening hours. I did not meet these men and they were never brought to our home.

After Ali nagged and nagged me to get pregnant, I agreed to stop taking birth control pills. Two months later we had an enormous fight and I decided that I was going to leave him. I had been feeling slightly sick during the week before the fight, so I went to my doctor. The doctor gave me a pregnancy test and I received a call from his office three days later. I could not leave Ali now; I was pregnant.

When I told Ali the news, he was extremely happy. I believe he knew I was thinking of leaving him, and he had not become a citizen of the United States yet. He understood that if I divorced him, without any children, he would not be able to attain citizenship and might have to return to Pakistan. I did not understand it at the time, but his main objective in marrying me was to become a citizen. After receiving citizenship he could begin to bring relatives over to America from Pakistan without having any trouble with immigration.

I gave up my thoughts of divorce and believed that I could make the marriage work if I just tried more to accommodate my Pakistani husband. My attitude changed and I thought how wonderful it would be to have a child. In Pakistan the only children acceptable to Muslim men were boys. So both Ali and I began to wish openly for a boy to be born. As I grew fatter and my belly enlarged I continued to have my pre-natal visits with my doctor. During one visit the OB/GYN announced that I was getting larger than a mother should be with only one child, so he listened to my abdomen with his stethoscope. He thought he heard two heartbeats, so he decided to do an X-ray.

I was pregnant with twins. I remember viewing the X-ray results and there were two tiny skeletons and two tiny skulls that showed up in the X-ray. Twins seemed the normal way to have children; after all, I was a twin and my sister was my best friend. In those days doctors could not tell the sex of the child before birth, so we waited, hoping for boys. Twin boys would have been quite an advantage for Ali so that he could brag to all of his relatives in Pakistan about being very virile. His brother had 11 boys, but no twins.

Throughout my pregnancy I continued to attend my classes at the university, walking all over campus, and working hard to finish all course work successfully before the children were born. They were due in February, 1972. I stopped school after the end of fall semester, in early December, 1971.

I went into labor on February 27th about 9:30 in the morning. I called my doctor and he said to wait until the contractions were closer together. Ali and I decided to go to my parents' home to wait. I packed my bag and we drove to their new house on the other side of Kirkwood. I waited all day as the contractions got closer and closer together. I was not allowed to eat, but could drink water or soda while waiting. About 6:00 o'clock in the evening, the doctor told us to drive to the hospital. Then we waited even more. I had chosen not to have my mother with me during labor, and in those days men were not allowed in the labor room.

At approximately 8:30 that night I was rushed into the operating room and the babies were delivered safely. They were beautiful girls. I was thrilled, but Ali stood in shock and disappointment. Girls in any Pakistani family were a curse. The father of girls has to pay for extravagant weddings and give gold jewelry as a dowry to the husband when they were married. I am sure Ali believed he was staring at total poverty when he looked at his two baby daughters.

I was taken back to a post partum room in the hospital and my girls were brought to me after they had been examined by a pediatrician. They were little bundles of joy and I loved them immediately. Ali scowled at them and became irritated that I enjoyed holding and kissing my daughters. I think the only thing that comforted him was that now he had children who were American citizens and that secured his place in America. My parents visited me that evening and saw the girls, too. Of course, my parents believed my children to be the most perfect babies ever born.

I don't believe Ali told his brother, sister, or mother that he had fathered girls for many months afterward. It was a great humiliation for him to tell his family that he had twin daughters. He once told me that when the doctor said the children were girls he felt like he had been run over by a truck.

CHAPTER 17: MORE TROUBLE

The weeks after my daughters were born left me worn out and depressed. Ali had numerous ways of showing his displeasure about the babies. He would not help with their feedings or changing their diapers, and I had many sleepless nights taking care of the girls. We named them Farah and Rani, two very Pakistani names meaning joy and cheerful in Urdu. Ali went to work during the day and he gambled at night when he was able to arrange a card game. Occasionally he would hold the girls and speak to them in Urdu to try to calm them down when they had colic, but usually he left their care to me. I got used to holding two children and after several months was able to begin feeding them cereal, which filled their tummies and made them sleep longer. I cleaned house, washed clothes, cooked, and played with the children during the day. They were my beloved daughters and we closely bonded with each other.

Approximately six months later I started having pains in my right side after I ate spicy or fatty foods. It was a gallstone attack, and my physician suggested an operation to remove my gallbladder. I waited as long as I could, but the doctor was afraid of complications, so during Christmas vacation, when Ali had two weeks off from his job, I went into the hospital for surgery.

My mother taught high school so she could not help take the children during the week and it became Ali's sole responsibility to serve as parent when I was in the hospital.

Before the girls were one year old I was gone for over seven days in the hospital, and when I returned from my surgery, they did not know me and cried when I held them. Their crying broke my heart. I was not allowed to pick anything up over 20 pounds, and by this time they were heavier than that weight. So I had to do the best I could with little babies when Ali returned to work in early January 1973.

We survived, but I know that Ali resented my mother for not helping more at that time. In Pakistan all female relatives would have pitched in to help and my mother did not do so more than once during the week I was in the hospital. My twin sister lived in Cairo, Illinois at this time and was not able to help with the children. In America, everyone works and cannot be expected to abandon their own life in order to help a perfectly capable man take care of his own children.

As the girls grew, we decided we needed to look for a house and move out of the apartment. We found one near the community college that had two bedrooms and purchased it. We moved into our small house when the babies were almost two years old.

Ali increased his gambling and was gone often at night during this time. Once when I questioned his gambling habits, he struck me hard across the face with his fist. I never again asked him to explain his hours away from the house. I stayed home with the girls and started a garden in the back yard. My small daughters and I made friends with other families on the block and young mothers who also stayed home to be with their children.

Soon I began to notice extra audio visual equipment stored in our basement. There were projectors, tape recorders, a large projection screen, and other equipment that belonged to the college. When I asked Ali about these items and why we had them in our house, he just brushed my questions aside and refused to answer me. He sold these items later by stripping off identifying marks and hocked them for extra money to use when he gambled.

I also saw Ali do his Muslim prayers more often during these days, and after his prayers he would make comments that he could put a curse on anyone who did not agree with him or tried to do him harm. He finally told me that he was having trouble at work with his boss, the woman vice president of the department. He said that a hearing was being held at the college to determine if he was to keep his job.

I was not allowed at the hearing, but when he returned from it he told me his version of the proceedings. The woman vice president accused him of not keeping an exact inventory of equipment, of not answering her questions truthfully, and not looking at her directly when he spoke to her. His excuse to the college personnel department director, who held the hearing, was that in Pakistan a man did not look into a woman's eyes who were not his wife. It was considered disrespectful to the woman. He received six months probation and was told if things did not get better he would be fired.

During this time I was getting very unhappy and wanted something else to do, so I decided to try to find a job. I had the girls at home alone with me all the time, so the obvious choice was for me to see if I could teach in a daycare center where the girls could attend class. I did find a job and the girls and I left home every day to go to the daycare center. I taught in one classroom and the girls attended daycare in another room. We would see each other on the playground and they would run to me and hug me. We stayed at that daycare center during the winter months of 1975 and early 1976.

Circumstances at the community college did not get any better and Ali decided that we would leave Kirkwood and move to Carbondale, Illinois so that he could finish his Ph.D. at the University. This move excited me and I was happy to move to Carbondale because I could attend the university also and go to graduate school.

Ali resigned and we put our house up for sale, sold it quickly, and moved to Carbondale, Illinois during the summer of 1976. Ali was immediately admitted to graduate school to finish his Ph.D. and I applied to be admitted to the education department as a graduate student. Southern Illinois University looked over my University of the Punjab degree, the SIU hours I had taken before getting married to Ali, and the University of Missouri hours, and decided that with a few additional undergraduate hours I could enter graduate school. I was given a job as a graduate assistant and worked as the director of the campus daycare center because of my experience teaching in the Kirkwood daycare center. I was happy with this lucky development.

We moved into student housing immediately off campus and both of us started graduate school. Life on campus was wonderful, stimulating, and filled the day with learning and American friends. Ali was busy with his own education and I had time away from the children, who were in preschool, and away from my Pakistani husband's tyranny.

Because I was director of the campus daycare center I had to make sure all parents paid their school fees, keep track of the school schedule and teachers covering the various classes. With my studies and my work at the daycare center I would be up in the evenings until late working on the center's financial records and studying for my classes. My daughters would come home in the afternoon, play outside for a short while, then eat dinner and fall asleep in front of the television on pillows. Ali would often work at the university library until late at night or he would gamble with his Indian and Pakistani friends whom he could easily cheat while playing card games.

Occasionally Ali would demand to have sex with me late at night, but I was not interested in any of his physical advances. Things had gone too far in my new found freedom around campus, and I had a better life to look forward to in the future without him. I would ignore his requests and pretend I was asleep so that he left me alone. His lifestyle disgusted me and, because of the university life, I was able to see that I did not need him anymore to take care of me. I believe he was having affairs with young female students who were in his classes at the university, too, but I really did not care about that situation. My only thoughts were how I could get away from him and take the girls with me so we could live on our own. Cheap housing was scarce and I was already living in one of the few apartments available. Moving out would have been difficult for me and I was still afraid of standing up to Ali.

One night while I was working late at my desk in the small living room area of the apartment, Ali came in with a bottle of wine in his hand. He decided that it was time for me to quit work, have a drink, and make love to him. I had finished the dishes from dinner earlier and put everything in the kitchen away afterward – so the kitchen counters were clean and neat. I had no intention of stopping my studies to have a glass of wine. So I declined the wine and refused to stop working at my desk. This made Ali so outraged that he put the wine down on a table and came to my desk yelling. He hit me savagely across the face with his hand and grabbed my hair, which was in a pony tail. Holding my long hair firmly he dragged me across the floor, while he beat me with his other hand. Pulling me toward the kitchen, I sensed he was searching for a knife to stab me with, but I had put them all in drawers earlier in the evening. It is funny how little things like cleaning the kitchen can make a difference in your life in moments of trouble, but I believe washing those dishes probably saved my life that night. I finally fought back and was able to break his firm hold on my hair. I ran to the front door of the apartment and flung it open, screaming for help.

He immediately knew that he could not hurt me or his own career would be ruined. The neighbors had already called the campus police and they arrived now at the entrance to the building. I stayed at the open door while the officers ordered him to get some belongings and leave the apartment. He went into the bedroom, packed a bag, and came out carrying two brown manila envelopes in one hand while his suitcase was in his other hand. I did not know it at the time, but he had gone into my jewelry box and taken all of the gold jewelry that I had brought back from Pakistan years before. The 22 karat gold bracelets, rings, and necklaces were in those manila envelopes. In his culture this jewelry belonged to him and he would keep it for his next wife when I had divorced him.

The police escorted him out of the apartment and I locked the door behind him. I then collapsed into a chair crying. I don't remember how I slept that night. My arm and back were badly bruised, but no bones were broken. The pain in my side and arm was tremendous, and I stayed awake thinking about what to do. During the entire evening and the fight with Ali neither daughter woke up or cried. They never knew what exactly happened to make Ali leave that evening, and I did not tell them until years later.

The next morning I looked in the phone book for divorce attorneys and found one who would see me that afternoon. I showed the attorney my bruises and cuts and he took photos and filed a restraining order again Ali. The Sheriff who served the restraining order found him staying at one of his Pakistani friends' houses within a few days.

After Ali received the restraining order and divorce papers he would often called me on the phone and harass me by saying all sorts of bad things concerning my behavior as a wife. I did not fit into the well behaved, Muslim, Pakistani mold that he believed I should. When I would mention the Kirkwood College's audio visual equipment he had stolen and his many lies, numerous card games and cheating, he would hang up the phone on me.

Ali didn't want the divorce. He fought it with his own lawyer and accused me of being unfaithful. During these months of fighting and threats I lost weight from the stress and got very ill with some type of fever. I visited the university medical center with a fever of 104 degrees, and the doctors wanted to keep me there in their small infirmary for a few days while they pumped me with antibiotics and aspirin trying to keep the fever down. A neighbor kept my children over night until someone could pick them up from her apartment. My mother drove down from Kirkwood to take my daughters back with her so they would stay for a few days until I recovered. While I was in the infirmary with this illness Ali visited me and started yelling so loud that the nurses had to have him escorted out of the building by the security guards. After a few days I was able to return home, and on the weekend I drove up to Kirkwood to pick up my daughters.

When the divorce was final Ali was ordered to pay 25% of his income per month and the girls' medical insurance. For months he refused to pay anything and I took him back to court to make him to live up to the divorce agreement.

I was living on my own and working to raise the girls, finish my education, and earn my Master of Science degree in Education. During the next two years I worked very hard, lived in university housing, and would even try to date occasionally. It is hard to live alone raising young girls, but they had good schools and I had good friends during this time. Ali would see them occasionally during this time and they would always come home with stories of his card playing and friends he socialized with during their visits.

Life has a way of working out and as the girls grew older I found someone to love and marry. A school teacher who taught my daughters in the new Carbondale kindergarten asked me on a date and we began to see each other often. Over time my boyfriend and I both graduated with our Masters Degrees in Education from Southern Illinois University, we got married, and moved out west with my two daughters.

EPILOGUE

Several years after our divorce, Ali pursued and married a Pakistani woman Pediatrician who had lived in America for many years. Within six months of being married to him she filed for divorce. I heard that he later went back to Pakistan, married a very young uneducated girl from Lahore, and then returned to the United States with her. They settled in the Chicago area and she gave birth to a baby girl. About three years after the girl was born they also had a baby boy.

Ali would send $200 child support monthly, until the girls were eighteen. For years I had tried to collect what he owed me in back child support payments and finally, when the girls entered college, the State of Colorado found Ali and worked a deal with the State of Illinois to collect that child support. He sent one last payment of $5,000 to me, and I used it to pay the girls college tuition for two semesters.

He never contributed to their medical insurance or any other medical related expenses. No presents, few greetings, and rare phone calls were made from him to his daughters. They visited him once when they were about eight years old and came home saying that he beat up his young wife in front of them so badly that the neighbors called police. After that they never wanted to visit him again. They changed their last names to my current husband's name and asked never to hear from Ali or see him again. They told stories of Ali threatening to take them to Pakistan and marry them to his cousins so that they were prisoners.

These stories frightened me, and I applied for their passports so that I could put the passports in a safe deposit box, in the hopes that this would prevent him from ever leaving the country with my daughters. I also learned how to shoot a handgun, and kept one in the house at all times. I was afraid that he would carry out his treats of stealing my daughters and take them to Pakistan where I would never be able to find them. I lived through years of fear that he could kidnap my daughters, and I would always take precautions to never allow him near the girls again.

Both daughters are happily married women now with families of their own. My fear of Ali has faded and now I realize that he treated me no differently than he would have treated any woman he married. He was from an ancient culture where he was raised to believe that women were possessions a man controls. Marrying me was a way for him to attain American citizenship and my feelings or my life did not matter to him. His purpose in marrying me was to use me, not because he loved me.

His basic understanding of life was formed when he was very young, in an old and conservative culture very different from the United States. His three Masters degrees, his Ph.D. degree, and his years of living and working in the United States did not change what he was taught in early childhood. His belief that he could lie, cheat, or steal to get what he wanted came from the culture and religion in which he was born.

I don't believe he is a unique person from many of his countrymen. I think that his conscience was never bothered when he cheated a non-Muslim and hurt a woman. He did what he believed he had to do to survive throughout his life, and his American education did not change his conservative Muslim values or behavior toward westerners.

As a young girl from Missouri, I mistakenly believed American culture and education would bring about a total change in a man from the Middle East. I now know that it is naive to expect someone brought up so differently from Americans to become suddenly westernized after only a few years in this country. People who are from regions of the world that still live with 16th century values, cultures, and beliefs will have these beliefs dominate their entire lives. When our politicians try to westernize or force democracy on Afghanistan, Pakistan, and Iraq they are not taking into consideration the cultures and traditions that these tribal people have lived with for hundreds of years.

About the Author

Lara was born in a small town in southeast Missouri to a middle class family. During her childhood her mother worked as an English teacher and her father a salesman. The family moved to Carbondale Illinois in 1965. After attending one year at Southern Illinois University, at eighteen years old, Lara met and then married a Pakistani man who was in his mid 30's. Within six months after the wedding, she traveled to West Pakistan and lived for almost two years as a Pakistani bride in Lahore. She returned to

America in 1970, gave birth to twin daughters in 1972 and divorced her Muslim husband in 1975. After her divorce she returned to school and finished her Master of Science Degree in Education. Her 30 year career as Director of Development and Executive Director for several large non-profit organizations has developed her skills in writing, public speaking, and management of organizations. She has studied world religions including Islam, Christianity, Hinduism, Buddhism, and Judaism in an effort to understand why people use religion to justify their actions toward others. Throughout her life she has traveled internationally and lived in St. Louis, Chicago, and Santa Fe, New Mexico. Lara is currently living on her ranch and raising money for a large hospital in a western state. She enjoys fishing, target shooting, farming, and raising horses. The Punjabi's Wife is her first book.

ALL THINGS THAT MATTER PRESS ™

FOR MORE INFORMATION ON TITLES AVAILABLE
FROMALL THINGS THAT MATTER PRESS, GO TO
http://allthingsthatmatterpress.com
or contact us at
allthingsthatmatterpress@gmail.com

4958718R0

Made in the USA
Lexington, KY
21 March 2010